# Crisco

## presents

# FAVORITE FAMILY FOODS

Cover illustration: Strawberry Glaze Pie; recipe on page 17.

© 1973 The Procter & Gamble Company
Cincinnati, Ohio

# Crisco presents
# FAVORITE FAMILY FOODS

—a collection of favorite recipes from Crisco's kitchens, especially chosen with hearty family appetites in mind. Favorite Family Foods is filled with recipe ideas for just about any occasion you might encounter in your daily living . . . popular menus to brighten up your daily meals . . . family favorites from the oven . . . dishes to please your pocketbook as well as your palate . . . even simple dishes for junior cooks.

Favorite Family Foods was created with you, your family and your busy schedule in mind. Throughout the pages that follow you will discover a variety of taste treats to enhance the many different food occasions in your family's life. Proven favorites as well as many new recipe ideas have been included in one easy reference that you'll want to keep handy.

Each featured recipe was carefully tested in our own kitchens and represents the same high quality which you have come to expect, and deserve, from Crisco. We hope that our favorite recipes will bring you and your family hours of eating pleasure and that our favorites will soon become your family's favorites, too.

*Luscious Deep Dish Apple Pie, page 19, Crisp Date Sugar Cookies, page 22, and Corn Stuffed Pork Chops, page 87 are all guaranteed to please your family.*

# FAMILY MENUS

Meals for your family need never be humdrum—after all, they're for your favorite people. Make them feel special by serving these delicious and nutritious menus. Each is exciting to serve because the meals are both attractive and tasty.

| MENU IDEA | Spanish Style Chicken<br>Onion Corn Muffins<br>Romaine-Tomato Salad | Banana Spice Cake<br>Fluffy Frosting<br>Coffee, Milk |
|---|---|---|

## SPANISH STYLE CHICKEN

1 frying chicken
  (2 1/2 to 3 pounds), cut up
1 teaspoon salt
1/4 teaspoon pepper
1/2 teaspoon monosodium
  glutamate
3 tablespoons Crisco
1/2 cup chopped onion
1 clove garlic, minced
1 cup tomato juice
2 cups chicken broth
1 cup uncooked long grain
  rice
1 package (10 ounces) frozen
  peas, broken apart
1/4 cup chopped pimiento

Season chicken with salt, pepper, and monosodium glutamate. In skillet, brown chicken in hot Crisco. Add onion and garlic; cook until onion is tender but not brown. Add tomato juice and 1/2 cup of the chicken broth; reduce heat. Cover; simmer 20 minutes. Add rice and remaining broth; stir so broth covers rice. Simmer, covered, 20 minutes. Add peas and pimiento. Simmer 5 minutes more or until peas are tender; stir once or twice. Makes 4 servings.

## BANANA SPICE CAKE

2 1/2 cups sifted cake flour
1 1/4 cups sugar
2 1/2 teaspoons baking powder
1/2 teaspoon baking soda
1 teaspoon salt
1 teaspoon cinnamon
1/2 teaspoon ground cloves
1/2 teaspoon nutmeg
2/3 cup Crisco
2/3 cup mashed banana
1/3 cup molasses
3 eggs
1/2 cup milk

In mixer bowl, combine flour, sugar, baking powder, soda, salt, spices, Crisco, banana, and molasses. Mix vigorously 2 minutes by hand or at medium speed of electric mixer. Add eggs and milk; beat 2 minutes more. Pour batter into 2 greased and floured 9x1 1/2-inch round layer pans. Bake at 350° for 35 to 40 minutes. Cool. Frost with Fluffy Frosting.

## FLUFFY FROSTING

1 1/2 cups sugar
1/8 teaspoon cream of tartar
1/2 teaspoon salt
2 egg whites
1 teaspoon vanilla

In top of double boiler, combine sugar, cream of tartar, salt, 1/3 cup water, and the egg whites. Place over boiling water and beat about 7 minutes with rotary beater or electric mixer until frosting holds stiff peaks. Mix in vanilla.

*Colorful, one-skillet Spanish Style Chicken is a grand way to start the week. A slice of avocado or a fluff of curly endive or parsley is a perfect garnish for this taste-tempting dish.*

| MENU IDEA | Sausage Breakfast Bake<br>Apple Maple Syrup | Baked Eggs<br>Grapefruit Juice, Coffee, Milk |
|---|---|---|

## SAUSAGE BREAKFAST BAKE

2 cups packaged pancake mix
1 1/4 cups milk
2 eggs
2 tablespoons Crisco, melted
1 jar (14 ounces) spiced apple rings
1 package (8 ounces) brown-and-serve sausage links

Combine pancake mix, milk, eggs, and Crisco; beat until nearly smooth with rotary beater. Pour into greased 13x9x2-inch baking dish. Drain apple rings; reserve syrup to use in Apple Maple Syrup. Halve each sausage link crosswise. Arrange apple rings and sausages over batter in pattern to be cut into 12 squares when served. Bake at 350° for 30 to 35 minutes. Serve with Apple Maple Syrup. Makes 6 servings.

## APPLE MAPLE SYRUP

Spiced apple syrup
1/3 cup sugar
4 teaspoons cornstarch
1 tablespoon butter or margarine
3/4 cup maple-flavored syrup

Add water to reserved apple syrup from Sausage Breakfast Bake to make 2/3 cup. In saucepan, combine sugar and cornstarch; stir in apple syrup. Cook and stir until thickened and bubbly; cook and stir 1 minute more. Stir in butter and maple syrup. Serve over Sausage Breakfast Bake. Makes 1 1/2 cups syrup.

## BAKED EGGS

6 eggs
Salt
Pepper
6 teaspoons milk

Butter 6 custard cups. Break one egg into each cup; sprinkle with salt and pepper. Add 1 teaspoon milk to each egg. Set cups in shallow baking pan; pour hot water into pan to depth of 1 inch. Bake at 350° for 25 minutes or until eggs are firm. Makes 6 servings.

## SUNBURST COFFEE CAKE

2 1/2 to 2 3/4 cups sifted flour
1 package active dry yeast
2/3 cup milk
1/4 cup Crisco
1/4 cup sugar
1 teaspoon salt
1 egg
1/2 teaspoon grated lemon peel
1/4 cup currant jelly

In large mixer bowl, combine 1 cup of the flour and the yeast. Heat milk, Crisco, sugar, and salt just until warm; stir to melt Crisco. Add to dry ingredients in mixer bowl. Add egg and lemon peel. Beat for 1/2 minute on low speed of electric mixer; scrape sides of bowl constantly. Beat 3 minutes at high speed. By hand, stir in enough of the remaining flour to make a moderately stiff dough. Turn out on lightly floured surface and knead until smooth and elastic, 3 to 5 minutes. Place in greased bowl; turn once to grease surface; cover and let rise until double, 1 to 1 1/2 hours. Punch down. Turn out on lightly floured surface; cover and let rest 10 minutes. Roll out to 10x8-inch rectangle, 1/2 inch thick. With doughnut cutter, cut into 12 doughnuts. Arrange the doughnut "holes" to make a solid circle in the center of a greased baking sheet. This forms coffee cake center. Stretch the doughnut rings slightly and arrange around doughnut holes. Let rise again until light, about 45 minutes. Bake at 375° for 12 to 15 minutes. Cool. Spoon currant jelly into center of outer rings. Drizzle with Confectioners Sugar Glaze, page 27. Sprinkle center of coffee cake with yellow sugar crystals.

*Spiced apple rings and brown-and-serve sausage links make Sausage Breakfast Bake special. Drizzle on Apple Maple Syrup to wake up appetites.*

| MENU IDEA | Orange Lamb Chops or<br>Hawaiian Pork Chops<br>Mixed Green Salad, Biscuits | Cherry Jubilee Pie or<br>Fudge Pudding<br>Coffee, Milk |
|---|---|---|

## ORANGE LAMB CHOPS

6 shoulder lamb chops, 3/4 inch thick
1/2 teaspoon grated orange peel
1/4 cup orange juice
1/2 teaspoon dried thyme
1 tablespoon Crisco
1 can (3 ounces) sliced mushrooms, drained

Trim excess fat from chops. Combine orange peel, juice, and thyme; spoon over chops. Let stand 1 hour at room temperature or several hours in refrigerator; turn chops once or twice. Drain, reserving orange mixture. Brown chops on both sides in hot Crisco; season with salt and pepper. Add orange mixture and mushrooms. Cover; simmer 40 minutes. Uncover; simmer 5 minutes more. Makes 6 servings.

## HAWAIIAN PORK CHOPS

4 to 6 pork chops
Salt
1/4 cup flour
1/2 cup Crisco
1 can (6 ounces) frozen pineapple juice concentrate, thawed
3/4 cup water
1 teaspoon sugar
1 teaspoon lemon juice
1/4 teaspoon cinnamon
1/4 teaspoon nutmeg
1 teaspoon cornstarch
1 tablespoon cold water
4 to 6 pineapple slices

Trim fat from chops. Sprinkle chops with salt; coat with flour. Brown chops on both sides in hot Crisco. Drain excess fat; add pineapple juice concentrate, the 3/4 cup water, the sugar, lemon juice, and spices. Simmer over low heat for 30 minutes. Combine cornstarch and the cold water; add to chops. Cook and stir until sauce thickens. Top each chop with pineapple slice; cook for 5 minutes more. Makes 4 to 6 servings.

## CHERRY JUBILEE PIE

1 Crisco pastry shell (9-inch)
1 can (21 ounces) cherry pie filling
2 tablespoons sugar
1/2 teaspoon cinnamon
1/4 teaspoon nutmeg
1 envelope whipped topping mix (2 to 2 1/2 cup yield)
1/4 cup sugar
1 cup dairy sour cream

Bake and cool pastry. Combine pie filling, the 2 tablespoons sugar, and the spices; set aside. Prepare topping mix according to package directions, except omit 2 tablespoons milk; beat to stiff peaks. Add the 1/4 cup sugar while beating at low speed. Gently fold in sour cream. Spoon half the cherry mixture into pastry shell; spread 2/3 of the topping mixture over the cherries; cover with remaining cherry mixture. Top each serving with dollop of remaining topping mixture and a maraschino cherry, if desired. Chill until firm, 2 hours. Store in refrigerator.

## FUDGE PUDDING

1 cup sugar
1/2 cup Crisco
2 egg yolks
2 squares (1 ounce each) unsweetened chocolate, melted and cooled
1/3 cup sifted flour
1 teaspoon vanilla
1/4 teaspoon salt
2 egg whites

Cream sugar, Crisco, and egg yolks. Add chocolate and mix well. Stir in flour and vanilla. Add salt to egg whites and beat until stiff; fold into chocolate mixture. Pour into greased 8x8x2-inch baking pan. Bake at 325° for 30 minutes. Serve warm with vanilla ice cream. Makes 6 to 8 servings.

*Orange Lamb Chops simmer in herbed orange juice for this weekday dinner. If your family prefers, make pineapple-sparked Hawaiian Pork Chops instead.*

| MENU IDEA | Shrimp Creole; Parsley Rice Ring | Blueberry Turnovers |
|---|---|---|
| | Dilly Bread | Coffee, Milk |

## SHRIMP CREOLE

1/2 cup chopped onion
1/2 cup chopped celery
1 clove garlic, minced
3 tablespoons Crisco
1 can (16 ounces) tomatoes
1 can (8 ounces) tomato sauce
1 1/2 teaspoons salt
1 teaspoon sugar
1 tablespoon worcestershire
  sauce
1/2 to 1 teaspoon chili powder
Dash bottled hot pepper sauce
2 teaspoons cornstarch
1 tablespoon cold water
12 ounces frozen shelled
  shrimp, thawed
1/2 cup chopped green pepper

In skillet, cook onion, celery, and garlic in hot Crisco until tender but not brown. Add tomatoes, tomato sauce, salt, sugar, worcestershire sauce, chili powder, and hot pepper sauce. Simmer, uncovered, for 45 minutes. Combine cornstarch with water; stir into sauce. Cook and stir until mixture thickens and bubbles. Add shrimp and green pepper. Cover; simmer 5 minutes. Spoon the hot Shrimp Creole into the center of the Parsley Rice Ring, or serve separately. Makes 6 servings.

## PARSLEY RICE RING

3 cups hot cooked rice
1/4 cup chopped parsley

Combine rice and parsley; pack into an ungreased 5 1/2-cup ring mold. Turn out at once on warmed platter. Makes 6 servings.

## DILLY BREAD

2 tablespoons chopped onion
1 tablespoon Crisco
2 1/2 cups sifted flour
1 package active dry yeast
2 teaspoons dill seed
  (or poppy, celery, or caraway
  seed)
1/4 teaspoon baking soda
1 cup cream-style cottage
  cheese, large curd
1/4 cup water
2 tablespoons sugar
1 teaspoon salt
1 egg

Cook onion in hot Crisco until tender. In mixer bowl, combine 1 cup of the flour, the yeast, dill seed, and soda. Heat together cottage cheese, water, sugar, and salt just until warm. Add to dry ingredients with the undrained cooked onion; add egg. Beat at low speed on electric mixer for 1/2 minute; scrape bowl constantly. Beat 3 minutes at high speed. By hand, stir in remaining flour. Cover; let rise until double, about 1 1/4 hours. Stir down. Turn into well-greased 9x5x3-inch loaf pan. Let rise until double and light, about 40 minutes. Bake at 350° for 50 to 55 minutes. Cover with foil the last 15 minutes. After baking, brush with softened butter and sprinkle with salt.

## BLUEBERRY TURNOVERS

Crisco pastry for 2-crust pie
1 cup fresh, frozen, or canned
  blueberries, drained
1/3 cup sugar
2 tablespoons flour
1 teaspoon lemon juice
1/8 teaspoon salt

Roll pastry to 1/8-inch thickness; cut in eight 5-inch squares. Combine blueberries, sugar, flour, lemon juice, and salt; place a heaping tablespoon on each square. Fold pastry in half diagonally; seal edges with fork. Cut slits for escape of steam. Place turnovers on baking sheet; bake at 400° for 20 to 30 minutes. Frost with Confectioners Sugar Glaze, page 27. Makes 8 turnovers.

*Molded Parsley Rice Ring is a snap to make to accompany our Shrimp Creole. Whip up some Raisin Muffins (page 31) if you don't have time for the Dilly Bread.*

| MENU IDEA | Ranch Round Steak | Peach Cobbler |
| | Texas Style Beans, Corn Bread Squares | Coffee, Milk |

## RANCH ROUND STEAK

3 pounds beef round steak,
  1/2 inch thick, cut in
  serving-size pieces
1/4 cup flour
2 teaspoons dry mustard
1 1/2 teaspoons salt
1/8 teaspoon pepper
1/4 cup Crisco
1/2 cup water
1 tablespoon worcestershire
  sauce

Trim excess fat from meat; slash edges to prevent curling. Combine flour, dry mustard, salt, and pepper; use to coat meat. Reserve remaining flour mixture. In skillet, brown meat, half at a time, on both sides in hot Crisco. Push meat to one side; stir in reserved flour mixture. Combine water and worcestershire; stir into skillet mixture. Cook and stir until thickened and bubbly; reduce heat. Cover and simmer for 1 to 1 1/4 hours or until meat is tender. Remove meat to warmed platter. Skim excess fat from gravy; drizzle gravy over meat. Makes 8 servings.

## TEXAS STYLE BEANS

2 cups pinto beans
1/4 pound salt pork, diced
1 cup chopped onion
1 clove garlic, minced
2 teaspoons salt
Dash pepper
2 cans (16 ounces each)
  tomatoes
3/4 cup diced green pepper
1 tablespoon sugar
6 drops bottled hot pepper
  sauce

In 2-quart bean pot or casserole, cover beans with water; soak overnight. Do not drain. Add salt pork, onion, garlic, salt, and pepper to the beans. Simmer, covered, for 2 hours. Add tomatoes, green pepper, sugar, and hot pepper sauce. Cover and simmer 3 hours more. Serve beans over Corn Bread Squares. Makes 8 to 10 servings.

## CORN BREAD SQUARES

2 eggs
2 cups buttermilk
3 tablespoons Crisco, melted
2 1/2 cups yellow cornmeal
1 1/2 teaspoons salt
1 teaspoon baking powder
1/2 teaspoon baking soda

Beat eggs until light; stir in buttermilk and melted Crisco. Combine remaining ingredients; beat into buttermilk mixture until batter is smooth. Pour into greased 9x9x2-inch baking pan. Bake at 425° for 25 minutes. Serve hot.

## ONION CORN MUFFINS

Add 1/2 cup chopped onion or 1/4 cup dried onion soup mix to corn bread batter. Pour batter into greased muffin pans. Bake as above.

## PEACH COBBLER

2 cans (16 ounces each)
  sliced peaches
1/3 cup sugar
1/2 teaspoon cinnamon
1/4 teaspoon nutmeg
2 tablespoons cornstarch
Drop Biscuits, page 30
1/3 cup sugar

In saucepan, combine peaches with syrup, the first 1/3 cup sugar, the spices and cornstarch; bring to boiling. Pour into ungreased 13x9x2-inch baking pan. Prepare Drop Biscuit dough, except add the remaining 1/3 cup sugar to the dry ingredients. Drop dough from tablespoon on hot peaches. Bake at 425° for 20 to 25 minutes or until top is lightly browned. Makes 6 to 8 servings.

*Transform your dinner table into a chuck wagon when you serve Ranch Round Steak and Texas Style Beans ladled over hot or cold Corn Bread Squares.*

Your family will feel like company when you serve German Beef Supper and hot Poppy Noodles. Shredded apples and carrots and dry red wine give this dish superb flavor.

| MENU IDEA | German Beef Supper, Poppy Noodles<br>Pumpernickel Bread | Apple Fritters<br>Coffee, Milk |
|---|---|---|

## GERMAN BEEF SUPPER

1 1/2 pounds beef stew meat, cut in 1-inch cubes
2 tablespoons Crisco
1 large apple, pared and shredded (1 cup)
1 medium carrot, shredded (1/2 cup)
1/2 onion, sliced
1/2 cup water
1/3 cup dry red wine
1 teaspoon salt or 1/2 teaspoon anchovy paste
1 clove garlic, minced
2 beef bouillon cubes
1 small bay leaf
1/8 teaspoon dried thyme
4 teaspoons cornstarch
1/4 cup cold water
1/4 teaspoon kitchen bouquet
4 cups medium noodles, cooked and drained
1/4 teaspoon poppy seed

Brown meat in hot Crisco. Add apple, carrot, onion, the 1/2 cup water, the wine, salt, garlic, bouillon cubes, bay leaf, and thyme. Cover and simmer for 2 hours or until beef is tender. Remove bay leaf. Combine cornstarch and the cold water; add to beef mixture. Cook and stir until thickened. Stir in kitchen bouquet. Serve over **Poppy Noodles**: combine hot noodles with poppy seed. Makes 4 servings.

## PUMPERNICKEL BREAD

2 3/4 cups stirred rye flour
3 packages active dry yeast
1 to 2 tablespoons caraway seed
1 1/2 cups water
1/2 cup dark molasses
2 tablespoons Crisco
1 tablespoon salt
2 to 2 1/2 cups sifted all-purpose flour
1 to 2 tablespoons cornmeal

In large mixer bowl, combine rye flour, yeast, and caraway seed. In saucepan, heat together water, molasses, Crisco, and salt just until warm; stir occasionally to melt Crisco. Add to dry ingredients in mixer bowl. Beat at low speed of electric mixer for 1/2 minute; scrape sides of bowl constantly. Beat 3 minutes at high speed. By hand, stir in enough all-purpose flour to make a stiff dough. Turn out on lightly floured surface; knead until smooth. Place in greased bowl; turn once to grease surface. Cover; let rise until double, 1 1/2 hours. Punch down; divide dough in half. Cover and let rest 10 minutes. Round each half into a smooth ball. Place on opposite corners of baking sheet sprinkled with cornmeal. Cover and let rise until double, about 30 minutes. Bake at 375° for 30 to 35 minutes or until well browned. For a chewy crust, brush tops of loaves with warm water several times during the baking after the first 20 minutes. Makes 2 loaves.

## APPLE FRITTERS

1 egg
1/2 cup milk
1 tablespoon Crisco, melted
1 cup diced pared apples or drained crushed pineapple
1 cup sifted flour
1 tablespoon sugar
1 teaspoon baking powder
1/4 teaspoon salt
Crisco for deep frying

Beat egg with milk; stir in the 1 tablespoon melted Crisco and the fruit. Combine dry ingredients; add to egg mixture and stir just until mixed. Drop from tablespoon into deep Crisco heated to 375°. Fry about 4 minutes, until brown and done in the center. Drain on paper toweling. Serve hot. If desired, roll in confectioners sugar. Makes 16.

# BAKING FAVORITES

**Home-baked treats are a favorite of everyone in the family. Some of the most popular pies, cookies, cakes, and breads are gathered on these pages. Why not pick one and treat your family today?**

## STRAWBERRY GLAZE PIE

1 Crisco pastry shell (9-inch)
6 cups fresh medium-size
  strawberries
1 cup water
3/4 cup sugar
3 tablespoons cornstarch
Red food coloring

Bake and cool pastry. Wash berries; remove hulls. Crush 1 cup of the smaller berries and cook with the water for about 2 minutes. Drain well with sieve; reserve juice. Add water if needed to make 1 1/4 cups juice. Discard cooked berries. In saucepan, combine sugar and cornstarch; stir in berry juice. Cook and stir over medium heat until thickened and clear. Stir in about 5 drops red food coloring. Spread a small amount of the glaze mixture (about 1/4 cup) on bottom and sides of baked pastry shell. Arrange half the whole berries, stem end down, in pastry shell. Spoon half the remaining glaze carefully over berries, being sure each is well coated. Arrange remaining berries, stem end down, on first layer; spoon on remaining glaze, coating each berry. Chill 3 to 4 hours. Garnish with whipped cream.

## BLUEBERRY PIE

Crisco pastry for 2-crust pie
4 cups fresh blueberries
3/4 to 1 cup sugar
3 tablespoons flour
1/2 teaspoon grated lemon
  peel
Dash salt
1 to 2 teaspoons lemon juice
1 tablespoon butter or
  margarine

Line 9-inch pie plate with pastry. In mixing bowl, combine blueberries, sugar, flour, lemon peel, and salt. Pour filling into pastry-lined pie plate. Drizzle with lemon juice and dot with butter. Place top crust on filling; cut slits for escape of steam; seal and flute edges. Bake at 400° for 35 to 40 minutes. If desired, sprinkle top crust with additional sugar.

## RHUBARB PIE

Crisco pastry for 2-crust pie
1 cup sugar
3 tablespoons flour
1 egg, beaten
2 cups rhubarb, chopped

Line 8-inch pie plate with pastry. Combine sugar and flour; add to beaten egg. Stir in rhubarb; pour into pastry-lined pie plate. Place top crust over filling; cut slits for escape of steam; seal and flute edges. Bake at 400° for 35 minutes.

## RAISIN PIE

Crisco pastry for 2-crust pie
2 cups raisins
1 1/2 cups water
1/2 cup sugar
2 tablespoons flour
1/2 cup chopped walnuts
1 teaspoon grated lemon peel
3 tablespoons lemon juice

Line 9-inch pie plate with pastry. In saucepan, combine raisins and water; cook, covered, for 10 minutes or until raisins are plumped. Combine sugar and flour; stir into raisins. Cook and stir over low heat until mixture thickens and bubbles. Cook 1 minute more. Remove from heat; stir in nuts, lemon peel, and juice. Pour hot raisin mixture into pastry-lined pie plate. Place top crust over filling; cut slits for escape of steam; seal and flute edges. Bake at 425° for 30 to 40 minutes.

*Strawberry Glaze Pie, featured on our cover, is one way to tell your family that you love them. Sparkly sweet glaze highlights each ruby-red whole berry.*

## APPLE PIE

Crisco pastry for 2-crust pie
6 large cooking apples
3/4 cup sugar
2 tablespoons flour
1 teaspoon cinnamon
1 tablespoon butter or
   margarine

Line 9-inch pie plate with pastry. Pare, core, and slice apples; place in pastry-lined pie plate. Combine sugar, flour, and cinnamon; sprinkle over apples. Dot with butter. Place top crust over apples; cut slits for escape of steam; seal edges. Bake at 400° for 30 to 40 minutes or until apples are tender and crust is golden brown.

## DUTCH APPLE PIE

Add 1/2 teaspoon nutmeg to sugar mixture in basic pie; combine with apples and 1/2 cup whipping cream. Proceed as above, topping pie with lattice top.

## CHEESE APPLE PIE

Substitute 1/2 cup shredded cheddar cheese for the cinnamon. Proceed as above.

## CHERRY PIE

Crisco pastry for 2-crust pie
1 cup sugar
1/4 cup flour
2 cans (16 ounces each)
   pitted tart red cherries
1/2 teaspoon almond extract

Line 9-inch pie plate with pastry. In saucepan, combine sugar and flour. Drain cherries, reserving 3/4 cup juice. Add cherries, the reserved juice, and the extract to sugar mixture. Cook and stir over medium heat until mixture thickens and bubbles; pour into pastry-lined pie plate. Place top crust over cherries; cut slits for escape of steam; seal and flute edges. Bake at 400° for 30 minutes or until crust is golden brown.

## CHERRY CRUNCH PIE

Prepare Cherry Pie as above. Before baking, combine 2 tablespoons flour, 1 tablespoon sugar, 2 tablespoons Crisco, and 1/4 teaspoon salt; sprinkle over top crust of pie. Bake as above.

## DEEP DISH PEACH PIE

3 cups sliced fresh peaches
   or 1 can (29 ounces) sliced
   peaches
1 cup water or peach syrup
2 tablespoons lemon juice
1 tablespoon cornstarch
Crisco pastry for 1-crust pie

In saucepan, combine peaches, water or peach syrup, lemon juice, and cornstarch; cook and stir over medium heat until thickened and bubbly, about 5 minutes. Pour mixture into 10x6x2-inch baking dish or 9-inch round or square baking dish. Roll pastry to 1/2 inch larger than top of dish; place over peaches. Flute edge and cut slits for escape of steam. Bake at 425° for 15 to 20 minutes. Makes 6 servings.

## DEEP DISH APPLE PIE

10 cups thinly sliced, pared
   apples (about 8 apples)
1 cup sugar
1 tablespoon flour
1/2 teaspoon cinnamon
1/4 teaspoon nutmeg
1/4 teaspoon salt
3 tablespoons butter or
   margarine
Crisco pastry for 1-crust pie

Place apples in 12x8x2-inch baking dish. Combine sugar, flour, cinnamon, nutmeg, and salt; sprinkle over apples; mix lightly. Dot with butter. Roll pastry into a rectangle about 1 inch longer and 1 inch wider than baking dish. Place over apples; flute edge and cut slits for escape of steam. Brush crust with milk; lightly sprinkle crust with sugar. Bake at 400° for 45 to 50 minutes. Serve warm with cream.

*Lattice-crusted Apple Pie served with a wedge of sharp cheese is an American tradition. One of its variations could become equally famous at your table.*

## LEMON MERINGUE PIE

1 Crisco pastry shell (9-inch)
1 cup sugar
1/4 cup flour
3 tablespoons cornstarch
1/4 teaspoon salt
2 cups water
3 egg yolks, beaten
1 tablespoon butter or
    margarine
1 teaspoon grated lemon peel
1/4 cup lemon juice
3 egg whites
6 tablespoons sugar

Bake and cool pastry. In saucepan, combine the 1 cup sugar, the flour, cornstarch, and salt. Stir in water. Cook and stir over medium heat until thickened and clear. Add a little hot mixture to egg yolks; return all to hot mixture. Cook 1 minute more; stir constantly. Remove from heat; blend in butter, lemon peel, and juice. Pour mixture into pastry shell. Beat egg whites until soft peaks form. Gradually add the 6 tablespoons sugar; beat to stiff peaks. Spread over hot filling. Bake at 425° for 5 minutes, until brown.

## CHOCOLATE MARSH-MALLOW PIE

1 Crisco pastry shell (9-inch)
16 large marshmallows
1/2 cup milk
1 bar (8 ounce) milk chocolate
    candy with almonds, broken
    in chunks
1 cup whipping cream

Bake and cool pastry. In top of double boiler, combine marshmallows and milk. Place over hot water; stir mixture until marshmallows melt. Add broken chocolate bar; stir until melted and smooth. Cool to room temperature. Whip cream; fold into marshmallow mixture. Turn into baked pastry shell. Cover with waxed paper or clear plastic wrap. Refrigerate at least 6 hours or overnight.

## CREAM PIE

1 Crisco pastry shell (9-inch)
1/2 cup sugar
3 tablespoons cornstarch
1/2 teaspoon salt
2-1/2 cups milk
3 egg yolks, beaten
1 tablespoon butter or
    margarine
1 teaspoon vanilla
3 egg whites
1/4 cup sugar

Bake and cool pastry. In saucepan, combine the 1/2 cup sugar, the cornstarch, and salt. Stir in milk. Cook and stir over medium-low heat until slightly thickened. Add a little hot mixture to egg yolks; return all to hot mixture. Cook until thickened, about 2 minutes. Stir in butter and vanilla. Pour mixture into pastry shell. Cool. Beat egg whites until soft peaks form. Gradually add the 1/4 cup sugar; beat to stiff peaks. Spread over filling. Bake at 425° for 5 minutes, until brown.

## CHOCOLATE CREAM PIE

Add 2 squares (1 ounce each) unsweetened chocolate to filling mixture after stirring in the milk. Proceed as above.

## BANANA CREAM PIE

Add 3 sliced bananas to filling before pouring into pastry shell. Proceed as above.

## SOUTHERN PECAN PIE

Crisco pastry for 1-crust pie
2 eggs, beaten
1 cup sugar
1 cup dark corn syrup
2 tablespoons butter or
    margarine, melted
1 teaspoon vanilla
1 cup pecans

Line 9-inch pie plate with pastry. Combine eggs, sugar, corn syrup, butter, and vanilla. Blend thoroughly; stir in pecans. Pour into unbaked pastry shell. Bake at 350° for 45 to 60 minutes, until knife inserted just off center comes out clean.

*Perfect Lemon Meringue Pie is sweet yet tart, has a creamy texture that holds its shape when cut, and is topped with a delectable golden-tipped meringue.*

## DOUBLE PEANUT BUTTER COOKIES

1 1/2 cups sifted flour
1/2 cup sugar
1/2 teaspoon baking soda
1/4 teaspoon salt
1/2 cup Crisco
1/2 cup creamy peanut butter
1/4 cup light corn syrup
1 tablespoon milk

Combine flour, sugar, soda, and salt. Cut in Crisco and peanut butter until mixture resembles coarse meal. Blend in syrup and milk. Shape in roll 2 inches in diameter; chill. Slice 1/8 to 1/4 inch thick. Place half the slices on ungreased cookie sheet; spread each with 1/2 teaspoon peanut butter. Cover with remaining slices; seal edges with fork. Bake at 350° for 12 minutes, or until browned. Makes 2 dozen.

## CHOCOLATE CHIPPERS

1/2 cup granulated sugar
1/4 cup brown sugar
1/2 cup Crisco
1 egg
1 teaspoon vanilla
1 cup sifted flour
3/4 teaspoon salt
1/2 teaspoon baking soda
1 cup (6-ounce package)
    semi-sweet chocolate chips
1/2 cup chopped nuts

Cream sugars, Crisco, egg, and vanilla. Combine flour, salt, and soda; stir into creamed mixture. Blend in chocolate chips and nuts. Drop from teaspoon 2 inches apart on greased cookie sheet. Bake at 375° for 10 to 12 minutes. Remove from sheet immediately. Makes 3 dozen.

## CRISP DATE SUGAR COOKIES

2 cups chopped dates
1/2 cup granulated sugar
1/2 cup water
1/4 teaspoon salt
2 tablespoons lemon juice
1 cup Crisco
1/2 cup granulated sugar
1/2 cup brown sugar
1 egg
3 tablespoons milk
1 teaspoon vanilla
3 cups sifted flour
1/2 teaspoon salt
1/2 teaspoon baking soda

In saucepan, combine dates, the first 1/2 cup granulated sugar, the water, and the 1/4 teaspoon salt. Bring to boiling; reduce heat, cover, and simmer about 5 minutes; stir frequently. Add lemon juice; cool. In mixer bowl, cream Crisco, the remaining granulated sugar, and the brown sugar. Add egg, milk, and vanilla; beat well. Combine remaining ingredients; add to creamed mixture and mix well. Chill at least 1 hour. On lightly floured surface, roll out half the dough to 1/8-inch thickness; cut with 2 1/2-inch round cutter. Transfer half the rounds to ungreased cookie sheet. Top each with 2 teaspoons date mixture. Top with remaining cookie rounds. Press edges together with tip of teaspoon to seal. Repeat with remaining half of dough. Bake at 375° for 10 to 12 minutes. Makes 3 dozen.

## OATMEAL QUICKIES

1 1/4 cups sugar
1/2 cup Crisco
2 eggs
1 1/2 cups rolled oats
1/2 cup sour milk or buttermilk
1 1/2 cups sifted flour
1 1/2 teaspoons baking powder
1/2 teaspoon baking soda
3/4 teaspoon salt
3/4 teaspoon cinnamon
3/4 teaspoon nutmeg
3/4 teaspoon ground cloves
3/4 cup raisins
3/4 cup chopped nuts

Cream sugar, Crisco, and eggs. Add oats and milk; mix thoroughly. Combine flour, baking powder, soda, salt, and spices; stir into oat mixture. Add raisins and nuts. Drop from teaspoon 2 inches apart on greased cookie sheet. Bake at 375° for 12 to 15 minutes. Makes 4 1/2 dozen.

*Bite into a Double Peanut Butter Cookie
and you'll find a creamy surprise—
a layer of peanut butter that's
baked right in the middle!*

Sunshine Cake, filled with cool
lemon filling, is a real treat. Sprinkle
snowy shreds of coconut all around it
for extra appeal.

## YELLOW CAKE

2 1/2 cups sifted cake flour
1 2/3 cups sugar
3 1/2 teaspoons baking powder
1 teaspoon salt
3/4 cup milk
2/3 cup Crisco
3 eggs
1/2 cup milk
1 teaspoon vanilla

In mixing bowl, combine flour, sugar, baking powder, and salt. Add the 3/4 cup milk and the Crisco. Beat vigorously by hand or at medium speed of electric mixer for 2 minutes. Add eggs, the 1/2 cup milk, and the vanilla. Beat 2 minutes more. Pour batter into 2 greased and floured 9x1 1/2-inch round layer pans. Bake at 350° for 40 minutes. Or bake 35 to 40 minutes in two 8x1 1/2-inch pans or a 13x9x2-inch pan.

## SUNSHINE CAKE

Bake Yellow Cake as above. Fill with **Lemon Filling:** In saucepan, combine 3/4 cup sugar, 2 tablespoons cornstarch, and dash salt. Add 3/4 cup water, 2 slightly beaten egg yolks, and 3 tablespoons lemon juice; cook and stir over medium heat until thickened. Remove from heat; add 1 teaspoon grated lemon peel and 1 tablespoon butter or margarine. Cool. Frost with Fluffy Frosting, page 5.

## MARBLE CAKE

Prepare batter for Yellow Cake. Pour 2/3 of batter into greased and floured 13x9x2-inch baking pan. Add 2 squares (1 ounce each) melted unsweetened chocolate and 1/4 cup sugar to remaining 1/3 of batter; blend well. Spoon chocolate batter here and there over yellow batter in pan. Pull knife through batter in wide curves several times to marble the cake. Bake at 350° for 35 to 40 minutes. Frost with Chocolate Frosting, page 27.

## SILVER CAKE

2 3/4 cups sifted cake flour
1 2/3 cups sugar
4 1/2 teaspoons baking powder
1 teaspoon salt
1 cup milk
2/3 cup Crisco
5 egg whites
1/3 cup milk
1 teaspoon vanilla

In mixing bowl, combine flour, sugar, baking powder, and salt. Add the 1 cup milk and the Crisco. Beat vigorously by hand or at medium speed of electric mixer for 2 minutes. Add egg whites, the 1/3 cup milk, and the vanilla. Beat for 2 minutes more. Pour batter into 2 greased and floured 9x1 1/2-inch round layer pans. Bake at 350° for 35 minutes. Or bake 35 to 40 minutes in two 8x1 1/2-inch pans or a 13x9x2-inch pan.

## SNOW BALLS

Prepare batter for Silver Cake as above. Pour batter into greased and floured 2 1/4-inch muffin pans. Bake at 375° for 15 to 20 minutes. Cool and spread with Fluffy Frosting, page 5, then roll in flaked coconut. Makes 2 1/2 dozen.

## CHOCOLATE CAKE

2 cups sifted cake flour
1 2/3 cups sugar
1 teaspoon salt
1 1/2 teaspoons baking soda
1/2 teaspoon baking powder
2/3 cup milk
1/2 cup Crisco
3 squares (1 ounce each)
  unsweetened chocolate,
  melted and cooled
3 eggs
2/3 cup milk
1 teaspoon vanilla

In mixing bowl, combine flour, sugar, salt, soda, and baking powder. Add the 2/3 cup milk, the Crisco, and melted chocolate. Beat vigorously by hand or at medium speed of electric mixer for 2 minutes. Add eggs, the remaining 2/3 cup milk, and the vanilla. Beat for 2 minutes more. Pour batter into two greased and floured 9x1 1/2-inch round layer pans. Bake at 350° for 40 minutes. Or bake 35 to 40 minutes in two 8x1 1/2-inch pans or a 13x9x2-inch pan.

## GRAND-MOTHER'S GINGERBREAD

1/2 cup brown sugar
1/2 cup Crisco
2 eggs
1/4 cup molasses
1 1/4 cups sifted flour
1/4 teaspoon salt
1 teaspoon baking soda
1/4 teaspoon baking powder
1 1/4 teaspoons ginger
1 teaspoon cinnamon
1/4 teaspoon ground cloves
1/2 cup hot water

In large bowl, combine brown sugar, Crisco, eggs, and molasses; blend well. Combine flour, salt, soda, baking powder, and spices; gradually blend into molasses mixture. Blend in hot water; pour batter into greased and floured 9x9x2-inch baking pan. Bake at 350° for 25 to 30 minutes. Serve warm with **Citrus Fluff:** In small saucepan, beat 1 egg; add 1/2 cup sugar, 1 teaspoon grated orange peel, 1 teaspoon grated lemon peel, and 2 tablespoons lemon juice. Cook and stir over low heat until thickened, about 5 minutes. Cool thoroughly. Fold in 1 cup whipping cream, whipped. Chill. Spoon onto squares of warm gingerbread. Garnish with a twist of orange.

## APPLESAUCE CUPCAKES

1 1/2 cups brown sugar
1/2 cup Crisco
1 egg
1 cup applesauce
1 teaspoon baking soda
1 teaspoon salt
1 teaspoon cinnamon
1/2 teaspoon ground cloves
2 cups sifted cake flour

Cream brown sugar and Crisco. Add egg and mix well. Combine applesauce and soda; stir into creamed mixture. Stir in salt and spices; add flour and mix thoroughly. Fill greased muffin pans half full. Bake at 400° for 15 minutes. Cool. Frost with Tangy Lemon Frosting, page 27. If desired, add 1/2 cup raisins or finely chopped nuts to batter before baking. Makes 18.

*Any time is the right time for warm squares of Grandmother's Gingerbread. Serve it with Citrus Fluff, vanilla ice cream, or applesauce.*

## VANILLA FROSTING

3 cups confectioners sugar
  (sift if lumpy)
1/4 cup Crisco
2 teaspoons vanilla
1/2 teaspoon salt
1/4 cup milk

In bowl, combine 1 cup of the sugar, the Crisco, vanilla, and salt. Alternately add milk and remaining sugar; mix until smooth and creamy. Add more sugar to thicken or milk to thin if needed for good spreading consistency. Frosts tops and sides of two 8- or 9-inch layers.

## CHOCOLATE FROSTING

1/4 cup Crisco
1/2 cup cocoa
1/4 teaspoon salt
1/3 cup milk
1 1/2 teaspoons vanilla
3 1/2 cups confectioners
  sugar (sift if lumpy)

In saucepan, melt Crisco. Remove from heat; stir in cocoa and salt. Mix in milk and vanilla. In mixer bowl, stir cocoa mixture into sugar. Beat at medium speed of electric mixer until smooth and creamy. Add 1 tablespoon more milk if needed for good spreading consistency. Frosts tops and sides of two 8- or 9-inch layers.

## TANGY LEMON FROSTING

3 cups confectioners sugar
  (sift if lumpy)
1/4 cup Crisco
1 tablespoon grated lemon peel
1/2 teaspoon salt
8 to 10 drops yellow food
  coloring (optional)
3 tablespoons water
1 tablespoon lemon juice

Combine 1 cup of the sugar, the Crisco, lemon peel, salt, and food coloring. Add water and lemon juice alternately with remaining sugar; mix until smooth and creamy. Add more sugar to thicken or water to thin if needed for good spreading consistency. Frosts tops and sides of two 8- or 9-inch cake layers.

## ORANGE FROSTING

3 1/2 cups confectioners
  sugar (sift if lumpy)
1/3 cup Crisco
2 tablespoons corn syrup
1 tablespoon grated orange
  peel
1/4 teaspoon salt
1/4 cup orange juice

Combine 1 cup of the confectioners sugar, the Crisco, corn syrup, peel, and salt. Alternately add the orange juice and the remaining confectioners sugar; mix until smooth and creamy. Add more sugar to thicken or juice to thin frosting if needed for good spreading consistency. Frosts tops and sides of two 8- or 9-inch layers.

## COCONUT PECAN FROSTING

2/3 cup sugar
2/3 cup evaporated milk
3 egg yolks
1/3 cup Crisco
1 1/3 cups flaked coconut
1 cup chopped pecans
1/2 teaspoon vanilla

In saucepan, combine sugar, evaporated milk, egg yolks, and Crisco. Cook and stir over medium heat until mixture comes to boiling. Remove from heat. Stir in coconut, pecans, and vanilla. Cool 15 minutes. For best results, spread only between layers and on top of cake.

## MAGIC COCONUT FROSTING

3/4 cup brown sugar
3/4 cup flaked coconut
1/2 cup chopped nuts
1/3 cup Crisco
2 tablespoons milk or cream
1/2 teaspoon salt

In saucepan, combine all ingredients. Cook and stir until sugar and Crisco are melted. Spread on partially cooled cake; bake at 400° for 6 minutes or until lightly browned.

## CONFECTIONERS SUGAR GLAZE

Milk or light cream
1 cup confectioners sugar
  (sift if lumpy)
1/2 teaspoon vanilla

Add enough milk, about 1 tablespoon, to confectioners sugar to make desired consistency. Add vanilla. Stir to blend well.

## PERFECT WHITE BREAD

5 1/2 to 6 1/2 cups sifted
   flour
2 packages active dry yeast
2 cups milk
1/4 cup Crisco
2 tablespoons sugar
2 teaspoons salt

In large mixer bowl, combine 2 1/4 cups of the flour and the yeast. In saucepan, heat together milk, Crisco, sugar, and salt just until warm; stir occasionally to melt Crisco. Add to dry ingredients in mixer bowl. Beat at low speed of electric mixer for 1/2 minute; scrape sides of bowl constantly. Beat 3 minutes at high speed. By hand, stir in enough of the remaining flour to make a soft dough. Turn out on lightly floured surface; knead until smooth. Place in greased bowl; turn once to grease surface. Cover; let rise until double, 1 to 1 1/2 hours. Punch down; divide dough in half. Shape in 2 loaves; place in 2 greased 9x5x3-inch loaf pans. Cover and let rise until double, 45 to 60 minutes. Bake at 400° for 45 minutes. Makes 2 loaves.

## CHEESE LOAF

2 1/2 to 3 cups sifted flour
1 package active dry yeast
1/2 cup shredded cheddar
   cheese
1 cup water
2 tablespoons sugar
2 tablespoons Crisco
1 teaspoon salt
1 egg

In large mixer bowl, combine 1 1/4 cups of the flour, the yeast, and cheese. In saucepan, heat water, sugar, Crisco, and salt just until warm; stir occasionally to melt Crisco. Add to dry ingredients in mixer bowl; add egg. Beat at low speed of electric mixer for 1/2 minute; scrape sides of bowl constantly. Beat 3 minutes at high speed. By hand, stir in enough of the remaining flour to make a soft dough. Turn out on lightly floured surface; knead until smooth. Place in lightly greased bowl; turn once to grease surface. Cover; let rise until double, 1 1/4 hours. Punch down; divide in half. Cover; let rest 10 minutes. Shape each half in roll 12 inches long. Twist the two rolls together in rope fashion; pinch ends together. Place in greased 9x5x3-inch loaf pan. Cover; let rise until double, 1 1/2 hours. Bake at 375° for 35 minutes. Makes 1 loaf.

## CARAMEL PECAN ROLLS

5 1/2 to 6 1/2 cups sifted
   flour
2 packages active dry yeast
1 3/4 cups milk
1/2 cup water
2 tablespoons granulated sugar
1 tablespoon salt
3 tablespoons Crisco
1 cup brown sugar
1/2 cup butter or
   margarine, melted
2 tablespoons corn syrup
1 cup pecan halves
4 tablespoons butter or
   margarine, softened
1/2 cup granulated sugar
1 teaspoon cinnamon.

In large mixer bowl, combine 2 1/2 cups of the flour and the yeast. In saucepan, heat together milk, water, the 2 tablespoons granulated sugar, the salt, and Crisco just until warm; stir occasionally to melt Crisco. Add to dry ingredients in mixer bowl. Beat at low speed of electric mixer for 1/2 minute; scrape sides of bowl constantly. Beat 3 minutes at high speed. By hand, stir in enough of the remaining flour to make soft dough. Turn out on floured surface; knead until smooth. Cover; let rest 20 minutes. Punch down. In saucepan, combine brown sugar, melted butter, and corn syrup. Cook and stir just until blended. Distribute evenly in bottom of 36 well-greased muffin pans (or three 9-inch round layer pans); top mixture with pecans. Divide dough in half; roll each to 10x6-inch rectangle. Spread with softened butter. Combine the 1/2 cup granulated sugar and the cinnamon; sprinkle over dough. Roll up, jelly-roll fashion, beginning with long side; seal edges. Cut into 1-inch slices. Place rolls, cut side down, in prepared pans. Cover; refrigerate 2 to 24 hours. Remove from refrigerator; let stand 20 minutes before baking. Bake at 425° for 20 to 25 minutes. Invert on racks. Makes 3 dozen.

No last-minute rolling and shaping for
these Caramel Pecan Rolls. You mix them
one day, then bake the next—they rise
feather-light in the refrigerator.

*Tender, flaky Biscuits make any meal unforgettable when served hot with plenty of butter and honey. Or try one of our tasty variations.*

## BISCUITS

2 cups sifted flour
3 teaspoons baking powder
1 teaspoon salt
1/3 cup Crisco
3/4 cup milk

In bowl, combine flour, baking powder, and salt. Cut in Crisco until mixture resembles coarse meal. Add milk; stir until blended. Transfer dough to lightly floured surface. Knead lightly, 8 to 10 times. Roll dough to 1/2-inch thickness. Cut with floured cutter. Bake on ungreased baking sheet at 425° for 12 to 15 minutes. Makes 16 biscuits.

## DROP BISCUITS

Increase milk to 1 cup; prepare dough as above. Drop from spoon on ungreased baking sheet.

## CHEESE BISCUITS

Stir 1/3 cup shredded sharp cheddar cheese into biscuit mixture before adding milk. Proceed as above.

## RAISIN BISCUITS

Stir 1/2 cup raisins into biscuit mixture before adding milk. Proceed as above.

## BISCUIT STICKS

Prepare biscuit dough as above; roll to 1/4-inch thickness. Cut in 5-inch strips; twist. Combine 1/4 cup sugar and 1 teaspoon cinnamon. Brush twists with melted butter; sprinkle with cinnamon mixture. Bake as above for 10 to 12 minutes.

## MUFFINS

2 cups sifted flour
2 tablespoons sugar
3 teaspoons baking powder
1 teaspoon salt
1 egg, slightly beaten
1 cup milk
3 tablespoons Crisco, melted

In bowl, combine flour, sugar, baking powder, and salt. Combine egg, milk, and Crisco; add all at once to dry ingredients. Stir quickly just until dry ingredients are moistened. Fill greased muffin pans 2/3 full. Bake at 400° for 20 to 25 minutes. Makes 12 muffins. Unmelted Crisco may be cut into dry ingredients, if desired.

## BLUEBERRY MUFFINS

Add 1 cup fresh or canned or frozen blueberries, drained, to muffin batter. Proceed as above.

## RAISIN MUFFINS

Add 3/4 cup raisins or finely chopped dates to dry ingredients. Proceed as above.

## COFFEE CAKE

3/4 cup sugar
1/3 cup Crisco
1 egg
1/2 cup milk
1 1/2 cups sifted flour
2 teaspoons baking powder
1/2 teaspoon salt

Combine sugar, Crisco, and egg; add milk and beat thoroughly. Combine flour, baking powder, and salt; stir into sugar mixture. Beat until smooth. Spread mixture in greased 9x9x2-inch baking pan; top with one of the following toppings. Bake at 375° for 30 to 35 minutes.

## ORANGE TOPPING

Combine 1/2 cup sugar, 1/3 cup flour, 2 tablespoons Crisco, and 2 teaspoons grated orange peel.

## COCONUT TOPPING

Combine 1/3 cup brown sugar, 1/3 cup flaked coconut, 1/3 cup chopped nuts, and 1 tablespoon Crisco.

## UPSIDE-DOWN COFFEE CAKE

2 cups sifted flour
1/4 cup sugar
3 teaspoons baking powder
1 teaspoon salt
1/3 cup Crisco
1 cup milk
1 egg

Combine flour, sugar, baking powder, and salt. Cut in Crisco until mixture resembles coarse crumbs. Add milk and egg; stir just enough to moisten the dry ingredients. Spread one of the following toppings in bottom of greased 8x8x2-inch baking pan; top with batter. Bake at 400° for 35 to 40 minutes.

## BLUEBERRY COFFEE CAKE

Combine 2 cups well-drained blueberries and 2 tablespoons grated orange peel in baking pan.

## CHERRY COFFEE CAKE

Combine 1 can (16 ounce) tart red cherries, drained (2 cups) and 1/4 cup sugar in baking pan.

## POPOVERS

2 eggs
1 cup milk
1 cup sifted flour
1/2 teaspoon salt
1 tablespoon Crisco, melted

Place eggs in mixer bowl; add milk, flour, and salt. Beat 1 1/2 minutes with rotary beater or at medium speed of electric mixer. Add melted Crisco; beat 30 seconds more. (Don't overbeat.) Fill 6 to 8 well-greased custard cups 1/2 full. Bake at 475° for 15 minutes. Reduce oven to 350° and bake 25 to 30 minutes more or until browned and firm. Before removing from oven, prick with fork to let steam escape. For dry and crisp popovers, turn off oven and leave popovers in oven 30 minutes with door ajar. Makes 6 to 8 large popovers.

## DINNER ROLLS

3 to 3 1/2 cups sifted flour
1 package active dry yeast
1 1/4 cups milk
1/4 cup sugar
1/4 cup Crisco
1 teaspoon salt
1 egg

In large mixer bowl, combine 1 1/3 cup of the flour and the yeast. Heat together milk, sugar, Crisco, and salt just until warm; stir occasionally to melt Crisco. Add to dry ingredients in mixer bowl; add egg. Beat at low speed of electric mixer for 1/2 minute; scrape sides of bowl constantly. Beat 3 minutes at high speed. By hand, stir in enough remaining flour to make a soft dough. Place in greased bowl; turn once to grease surface. Cover; let rise until double, 1 to 1 1/2 hours. Punch down; turn out on lightly floured surface. Cover; let rest 10 minutes. Shape as desired (see drawings). Cover and let shaped rolls rise until double, 30 to 45 minutes. Bake on greased baking sheet or in greased muffin pans at 400° for 12 to 15 minutes. Makes 2 dozen Butterfans, Crescents, Bowknots, or Cloverleafs.

## ORANGE ROLLS

Prepare 1/2 recipe Dinner Rolls as above including all steps through the 10 minute rest. On lightly floured surface, roll to 16x8-inch rectangle. Combine 1/4 cup sugar, 2 tablespoons melted butter, and 2 teaspoons grated orange peel; spread over dough. Roll lengthwise as for jelly roll. Seal edge; cut in 1-inch slices. Place cut side down in greased 9x9x2-inch baking pan. Cover; let rise until double, 30 to 40 minutes. Bake at 375° for 20 to 25 minutes. Remove from pan. Frost with Confectioners Sugar Glaze, page 27, if desired.

## REFRIGERATOR ROLLS

Prepare Dinner Rolls as above; do not let rise. Place dough in greased bowl; turn it once to grease surface. Cover; chill at least 2 hours, or up to 4 or 5 days. About 2 hours before serving, shape the dough as desired (see drawings) on floured surface. Cover; let rise until double, 1 1/4 hours. Bake as above.

## WHOLE WHEAT ROLLS

3 1/2 cups stirred whole
   wheat flour
2 packages active dry yeast
2 cups milk
1/2 cup sugar
1 tablespoon salt
3 tablespoons Crisco
2 eggs
3 1/4 to 3 1/2 cups sifted
   all-purpose flour

In large mixer bowl, combine whole wheat flour and the yeast. In saucepan, heat together milk, sugar, salt, and Crisco just until warm; stir occasionally to melt Crisco. Add to dry ingredients in mixer bowl; add eggs. Beat at low speed of electric mixer for 1/2 minute; scrape sides of bowl constantly. Beat 3 minutes at high speed. By hand, stir in enough all-purpose flour to make a soft dough. Turn out on lightly floured surface; knead until smooth. Place in greased bowl; turn once to grease surface. Cover; let rise until double, 1 1/2 hours. Punch down; cover and let rest 10 minutes. Shape in 24 rolls; place on greased baking sheets. Cover and let rise until almost double, 45 minutes. Bake at 400° for 15 to 20 minutes or until browned. Remove from baking sheets; cool. Makes 2 dozen.

One batch of Basic Roll Dough makes two dozen Butterfans, Crescents, Bowknots, or Cloverleafs. Brush with a swish of melted butter after baking for tender crusts.

## TIPS FOR BAKING IDEAL DINNER ROLLS

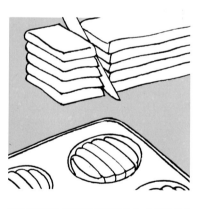

**Butterfans:** Roll dough to 27x 14-inch rectangle. Cut crosswise in 18 strips. Brush with melted butter. Stack 6 strips; cut in 9 portions. Place in muffin pans.

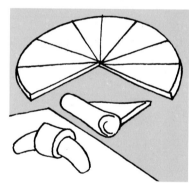

**Crescents:** Roll dough in two 12-inch circles. Brush with melted butter. Cut each in 12 wedges. Roll wedge toward point. Place point down on baking sheet; curve ends.

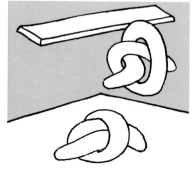

**Bowknots:** Roll dough to 18x 10-inch rectangle, 1/2 inch thick. Cut strips 10 inches long, 3/4 inches wide. Roll strips lightly under fingers; loosely tie knot.

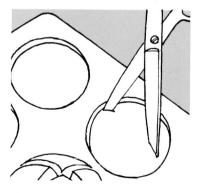

**Cloverleafs:** Divide dough into 24 pieces; form each into ball. Place each in a greased muffin pan. Snip each ball across top, making 2 deep cuts at right angles.

After baking, serve rolls at once or cool on racks away from drafts. To reheat, place rolls in paper bag; sprinkle bag with water; warm in 400° oven.

# CASSEROLES AND SKILLET DISHES

**Keep kitchen clutter to a minimum when you make these easy and appetizing dishes. Crisp salad fixings and a touch of dessert sweetness make your meal complete. What easier way to satisfy those hearty appetites?**

## MEAT 'N TATER PIE

Crisco pastry for 2-crust pie
1 pound ground beef
1/2 cup milk
1/2 envelope (3 tablespoons) dry onion soup mix
Dash pepper
Dash allspice
1 package (12 ounces) loose-pack frozen hash-brown potatoes, thawed

Line 9-inch pie plate with pastry. Combine meat, milk, soup mix, pepper, and allspice; mix gently. Lightly pat into pastry-lined pie plate; top with potatoes. Place top crust over potatoes; seal and flute edge. Cut design in top pastry. Bake at 350° for 1 hour, or until browned. Serve with warmed catsup, if desired. Makes 6 to 8 servings.

## CHILI MOSTACCIOLI

1 pound ground beef
1 cup soft bread crumbs
1/2 cup milk
1 teaspoon salt
Dash pepper
2 tablespoons Crisco
1/4 cup chopped onion
1 clove garlic, minced
2 cans (11 ounces each) condensed chili-beef soup
1 soup can water
7 ounces mostaccioli or tubular macaroni (3 cups)
Grated parmesan cheese

Combine meat, crumbs, milk, salt, and pepper; shape into five oblong patties. In skillet, brown patties in hot Crisco. Remove patties; set aside. Cook onion and garlic in same skillet until tender but not brown. Blend in soup and water. Return patties to skillet. Bring mixture to boiling; simmer, covered, for 15 minutes. Cook mostaccioli according to package directions; drain and place on large heated platter. Arrange patties on noodles. Pour sauce over meat; sprinkle with cheese. Makes 5 servings.

## ENCHILADA CASSEROLE

6 tortillas (frozen or canned)
Crisco for shallow frying
1 pound ground beef
1/2 cup chopped onion
1 can (10 1/2 ounces) condensed cream of mushroom soup
1 can (10 ounces) enchilada sauce
1 can (5 1/3 ounces) evaporated milk (2/3 cup)
1 cup (4 ounces) shredded sharp process American cheese
2 to 4 tablespoons chopped and seeded canned green chilies

Fry tortillas in hot Crisco until crisp, according to label directions. Drain on paper toweling; break into bite-size pieces. In skillet, cook beef and onion until beef is lightly browned. Stir in soup. Add remaining ingredients and tortillas; turn into 2-quart casserole. Bake at 350° for 1 hour. Stir once or twice while baking. Makes 6 servings.

*Ground beef does it again—featured this time in Meat 'n Tater Pie. Frozen hash-brown potatoes and zesty burger filling are nestled between pastry layers.*

## CHICKEN RICE CASSEROLE

1 chicken bouillon cube
1/2 cup Crisco
2 tablespoons flour
1 cup milk or light cream
3 cups diced cooked chicken
3 cups cooked rice
3/4 cup chopped celery
1/2 cup chopped onion
1 jar (2 ounces) pimientos,
   drained and chopped
1 tablespoon chopped parsley
1 teaspoon salt
1/2 teaspoon pepper
1/4 cup cornflake crumbs

Dissolve bouillon cube in 1 cup hot water. In skillet, melt Crisco; stir in flour. Add bouillon and milk gradually. Cook and stir over medium heat until thickened and bubbly. Add chicken, rice, celery, onion, pimiento, parsley, salt, and pepper. Pour into 2 1/2-quart casserole; sprinkle with cornflake crumbs. Bake at 350° for 25 to 30 minutes or until top is browned. Makes 8 servings.

## CHICKEN ALMOND

2 cups raw chicken breasts,
   sliced in strips
1/4 cup Crisco
2 cans (5 ounces each) bamboo
   shoots, drained and diced
2 cups diced celery
2 cans (5 ounces each) water
   chestnuts, drained and
   sliced
3 cups chicken broth
2 tablespoons soy sauce
1/3 cup cornstarch
1/2 cup cold water
1/2 cup almond halves, toasted

In large heavy skillet, quickly cook chicken in hot Crisco; use high heat and stir quickly. (Do not overcook.) Add bamboo shoots, celery, water chestnuts, chicken broth, and soy sauce; mix thoroughly. Bring to boiling; cover and cook 5 minutes over low heat, or until vegetables are crisp-tender. Combine cornstarch and cold water; add to chicken. Cook and stir until mixture thickens and bubbles. Salt to taste. Garnish with almonds. Serve immediately over hot cooked rice, if desired. Makes 6 to 8 servings.

## CHICKEN WITH ORANGE

1 frying chicken (2 1/2 to 3
   pounds), cut up
2 tablespoons Crisco
1 teaspoon salt
1/2 teaspoon paprika
1 medium onion, sliced
1/3 cup (3 ounces) canned
   frozen orange juice
   concentrate, thawed
1/3 cup water
2 tablespoons brown sugar
2 tablespoons chopped parsley
2 teaspoons soy sauce
1/2 teaspoon ginger

In skillet, brown chicken on all sides in hot Crisco; sprinkle with salt and paprika. Arrange onion over chicken. Combine juice concentrate, water, brown sugar, parsley, soy, and ginger; pour over chicken and onion. Cover and simmer until chicken is tender, 35 to 40 minutes. Serve over hot cooked rice if desired. Makes 4 servings.

## CHICKEN SKILLET

1/3 cup flour
1 teaspoon salt
1 teaspoon paprika
1/4 teaspoon ground sage
1/4 teaspoon pepper
1 frying chicken (2 1/2 to 3
   pounds), cut up
1/4 cup Crisco
1 teaspoon sugar
1 can (13 3/4 ounces)
   chicken broth
1 tablespoon lemon juice
1 cup sliced carrots
1 medium onion, sliced
2 tablespoons chopped parsley

Combine flour, salt, paprika, sage, and pepper in paper or plastic bag; add chicken, a few pieces at a time, and shake to coat. Reserve excess flour mixture. In skillet, brown chicken on all sides in hot Crisco. Remove chicken. Stir reserved flour mixture and sugar into pan drippings; add chicken broth. Cook and stir until thickened and bubbly. Stir in lemon juice, carrots, onion, and parsley. Return chicken to skillet. Cover and cook until vegetables and chicken are tender, 40 to 45 minutes; stir occasionally. Makes 4 servings.

One stewing chicken goes a long way when you make Chicken and Dumplings. For best results, be certain that chicken stock is boiling hot when you drop in the dumplings.

## CHICKEN & DUMPLINGS

1 stewing chicken
  (5 to 6 pounds), cut up or
  2 frying chickens, cut up
2 sprigs parsley
4 celery ribs with leaves
1 carrot, pared and sliced
1 small onion, cut up
2 teaspoons salt
1/4 teaspoon pepper
1 bay leaf
1 cup sifted flour
2 teaspoons baking powder
1/2 teaspoon salt
1/2 cup milk
2 tablespoons Crisco, melted
2 tablespoons chopped parsley

In Dutch oven or large kettle, add enough water to chicken to cover. Add parsley sprigs, celery, carrot, onion, the 2 teaspoons salt, the pepper, and bay leaf. Cover; bring to boiling and simmer 2 1/2 hours or until meat is tender. Combine flour, baking powder, and the 1/2 teaspoon salt. Combine milk and Crisco; add with chopped parsley to dry ingredients; stir just to moisten. Drop from tablespoon directly onto chicken in boiling broth. Cover tightly; return to boiling. Reduce heat (don't lift cover); simmer 12 to 15 minutes. Serve with **Chicken Gravy**: Strain the chicken broth; measure 4 cups into saucepan. Heat to boiling. Combine 1/2 cup flour and 1 cup cold water; gradually add to broth; mix well. Cook and stir until thickened. Add 1 1/2 teaspoons salt and dash pepper. Makes 6 to 8 servings.

## PAPRIKA CHICKEN

1/3 cup flour
1 teaspoon salt
Dash pepper
1 frying chicken (2 1/2 to 3
  pounds), cut up
1/4 cup Crisco
1/2 cup chopped onion
1/4 cup water
1 tablespoon paprika

Combine flour, salt, and pepper in bag; add a few pieces of chicken at a time and shake to coat. In skillet, brown chicken on all sides in hot Crisco. Add onion, water, and paprika. Cover; simmer 45 minutes. Remove chicken and keep warm. Serve with **Sour Cream Gravy**: Blend 1 tablespoon flour and 1/4 teaspoon salt into pan juices. Add 1/2 cup milk and 1/2 cup dairy sour cream. Cook and stir until thickened. Makes 4 servings.

Accompany this thrifty Tuna Broccoli
Casserole with crisp lettuce wedges and
bowls of chocolate pudding with tiny
marshmallows for a hearty family supper.

# TUNA BROCCOLI CASSEROLE

2 packages (10 ounces each) frozen chopped broccoli
6 tablespoons Crisco
1/2 cup flour
1 teaspoon salt
3 1/2 cups milk
1/3 cup grated parmesan cheese
2 tablespoons lemon juice
1/4 teaspoon dried dillweed
1 can (12 1/2 ounces) tuna, drained
1 package refrigerated biscuits (10 biscuits)

Cook broccoli according to package directions; drain. In large saucepan, melt Crisco over low heat; blend in flour and salt. Add milk all at once. Cook and stir until thickened and bubbly. Add parmesan, lemon juice, and dillweed. Stir in broccoli and tuna. Pour into 2-quart casserole. Bake at 375° for 30 minutes. Cut four refrigerated biscuits in quarters; arrange quarters around edge of hot casserole and bake 15 minutes longer. Makes 8 servings. Bake remainder of biscuits according to package directions.

# QUICK TUNA SKILLET

1/3 cup bias-cut celery slices
2 tablespoons Crisco
1 package (10 ounces) frozen peas and onions
1/2 cup water
2 tablespoons soy sauce
2 teaspoons cornstarch
2 cups cooked rice
1 can (12 1/2 ounces) tuna, drained
1 can (5 ounces) water chestnuts, thinly sliced

In skillet, cook celery in hot Crisco until tender; add frozen peas and onions, and water. Heat to boiling. Cover and simmer until peas are tender, 8 to 10 minutes. Combine soy and cornstarch; add to vegetables. Cook and stir until thickened and bubbly. Gently stir in remaining ingredients; heat. Serve with extra soy, if desired. Makes 4 servings.

# TUNA AU GRATIN PIE

Crisco pastry for 1-crust pie
1 can (10 1/2 ounces) condensed cream of mushroom soup
1/3 cup chopped onion
1/4 cup milk
2 tablespoons flour
1 package (10 ounces) frozen peas, thawed and drained
1 can (12 1/2 ounces) tuna, drained
2 tablespoons chopped pimiento
1 cup (4 ounces) shredded sharp process American cheese

Line 9-inch pie plate with pastry; trim crust; prick bottom and flute edge. Place extra pieces of dough on baking sheet. Bake pastry shell and extra pieces at 425° for 12 minutes or until lightly brown. When cool, crumble pastry pieces. In saucepan, combine soup, onion, milk, and flour. Cook and stir until thickened and bubbly. Remove from heat; stir in peas, tuna, and pimiento. Pour into pastry shell; top with cheese and pastry crumbs. Bake at 425° for 12 to 15 minutes, until cheese melts. Makes 6 to 8 servings.

# FRENCH ONION PIE

Crisco pastry for 1-crust pie
1 can (3 1/2 ounces) French fried onions
4 eggs, slightly beaten
2 cups milk
1 1/2 cups (6 ounces) shredded sharp process American cheese
1/2 teaspoon salt
Dash cayenne

Line 9-inch pie plate with pastry; prick bottom and flute edge. Bake crust at 450° for 7 to 8 minutes or until golden; remove from oven. Reduce oven temperature to 325°. While pastry is still warm, fill bottom with 1 1/2 cups of the French fried onions; reserve remainder. Combine eggs, milk, 1/2 cup of the cheese, the salt, and cayenne; pour into pastry shell and sprinkle with remaining cheese. Bake at 325° for 45 minutes; sprinkle reserved onions around edge. Bake 5 to 10 minutes more or until knife inserted just off center comes out clean. Let stand at room temperature 10 minutes before serving. Makes 6 servings.

*Add extra appeal to left-over stew by arranging Buttermilk Biscuits on top. Use your own favorite stew for the base of this Beef Pie, or try our version of Hearty Beef Stew.*

## BEEF PIE &
## BUTTERMILK
## BISCUITS

1 1/2 cups sifted flour
1 1/2 teaspoons baking powder
1/2 teaspoon salt
1/4 teaspoon baking soda
1/4 cup Crisco
1/2 cup buttermilk
1/2 recipe Hearty Beef Stew

Combine dry ingredients; cut in Crisco until mixture resembles coarse meal. Add buttermilk; stir until dough holds together. Transfer dough to lightly floured surface. Knead lightly, 8 to 10 folds. Roll dough to 1/2-inch thickness. Cut with floured cutter. Heat beef stew until bubbly; pour into 2-quart casserole or oven-proof skillet. Place biscuits atop. Bake at 425° for 12 to 15 minutes. Makes 4 to 6 servings.

## HEARTY BEEF
## STEW

2 pounds beef chuck, cubed
1/4 cup flour
1/4 cup Crisco
4 cups water
1 can (8 ounces) tomato
   sauce
1/4 cup chopped onion
1/2 teaspoon garlic salt
1 bay leaf
2 teaspoons salt
1/4 teaspoon pepper
6 medium potatoes, pared and
   quartered
6 medium carrots, pared and
   cut in 1-inch pieces
3 medium onions, quartered
1/4 cup cold water
1/4 cup cornstarch

Coat beef cubes with flour. In Dutch oven, brown meat in hot Crisco. Add the 4 cups water, the tomato sauce, the chopped onion, garlic salt, bay leaf, salt, and pepper. Bring to boiling; reduce heat. Cover and simmer 1 1/2 to 2 hours or until meat is tender. Add potatoes, carrots, and quartered onions; cover and simmer 50 to 60 minutes or until vegetables are tender. Combine cold water and cornstarch; stir into meat mixture. Cook and stir until mixture thickens, about 5 minutes. Remove bay leaf. Makes 8 to 10 servings.

## SIMMERED BEEF SHANKS

2 tablespoons flour
1 tablespoon salt
1/4 teaspoon pepper
3 to 4 pounds crosscut beef shanks
1 tablespoon Crisco
1 cup tomato juice
2 tablespoons chopped parsley
1/2 teaspoon dried basil
4 medium potatoes, pared and quartered
1/2 cup cold water
2 tablespoons flour

Combine the first 2 tablespoons flour, the salt, and pepper in paper or plastic bag; add beef shanks, one at a time, and shake to coat. In Dutch oven, brown meat in hot Crisco. Add tomato juice, parsley and basil. Cover and simmer 1 1/2 hours. Add potatoes; cover and simmer 30 to 45 minutes more or until potatoes are tender. Remove meat and potatoes to warmed platter; skim off excess fat from pan juices. Add enough water to juices to make 1 cup liquid. Combine the cold water and the remaining 2 tablespoons flour; stir into juices. Cook and stir until thickened and bubbly. Serve with meat and potatoes. Makes 4 to 6 servings.

## SPEEDY STROGANOFF

1 pound beef sirloin, cut in narrow strips
1 tablespoon Crisco
1 medium onion, sliced
1 clove garlic, minced
1 can (10 1/2 ounces) condensed cream of mushroom soup
1 cup dairy sour cream
1 can (3 ounces) sliced mushrooms, undrained
2 tablespoons catsup
2 teaspoons worcestershire sauce

In skillet or blazer pan of chafing dish, brown meat strips in hot Crisco. Add onion and garlic; cook until onion is crisp-tender. Combine soup, sour cream, mushrooms, catsup, and worcestershire; pour over meat. Cook and stir over low heat until hot. Keep warm over hot water. Serve over **Poppy Noodles**: Toss 4 cups hot cooked noodles with 1 tablespoon butter and 1 teaspoon poppy seed. Serve meat mixture over poppy noodles on platter. Makes 4 servings.

## BEEF POT ROAST IN BEER

3-to 4-pound beef rump roast
2 tablespoons flour
1 teaspoon salt
Dash pepper
2 tablespoons Crisco
1 can (12 ounces) beer
2 bay leaves
6 small whole onions
4 medium carrots, pared and cut in 1-inch pieces
1/2 cup cold water
1/4 cup flour
2 tablespoons catsup

Coat roast with 2 tablespoons flour. Season with salt and pepper. In Dutch oven or large skillet, brown roast on all sides in hot Crisco. Add 1/2 cup of the beer and the bay leaves. Cover tightly; simmer 1 1/2 hours. Remove bay leaves. Add onions and carrots. Cook 1 hour more or until meat and vegetables are tender; remove to heated platter. Skim fat from pan juices. Add enough of the remaining beer to make 1 1/2 cups liquid. Combine cold water and remaining 1/4 cup flour; stir into juices with the catsup. Cook and stir until thickened and bubbly. Season to taste. Cook and stir 2 to 3 minutes more. Makes 6 to 8 servings.

## CURRIED BEEF CUBES

2 pounds beef chuck, cut in 3/4-inch cubes
1/3 cup flour
1/3 cup Crisco
1 large onion, sliced
2 cans (8 ounces each) tomato sauce
1 1/2 cups water
1 clove garlic, minced
1 teaspoon salt
1/4 teaspoon pepper
2 teaspoons curry powder
1 package (9 ounces) frozen cut green beans
Hot cooked rice or noodles

Coat beef cubes with flour. In skillet, brown meat in hot Crisco. Add onion; cook until tender. Combine tomato sauce, water, garlic, salt, and pepper; pour over meat. Cover and simmer 1 1/2 hours or until meat is tender. Stir in curry powder. Add beans; cook until tender, about 15 minutes. Separate beans with fork as they heat. Serve over hot rice or noodles. Makes 6 to 8 servings.

## ORIENTAL SKILLET SUPPER

1 cup green pepper strips
2/3 cup bias-cut celery
   slices
2 tablespoons Crisco
2 large or 4 small
   tenderized pork cutlets,
   cut in 1/4-inch strips
2/3 cup cold water
2 tablespoons soy sauce
4 teaspoons cornstarch
1 teaspoon sugar
1/2 teaspoon salt
2 medium tomatoes, peeled
   and cut in wedges
2 cups hot cooked rice
1/2 teaspoon ginger

In heavy skillet, quickly cook green pepper and celery in hot Crisco until crisp-tender. Remove and set aside. Add meat to hot skillet; brown quickly. Combine water, soy sauce, cornstarch, sugar, and salt; add to skillet. Cook and stir until mixture thickens and bubbles. Add celery, green pepper, and tomatoes; heat through. Serve over **Ginger Rice:** toss hot rice with ginger. Serve extra soy sauce, if desired. Makes 4 servings.

## HAM & CHEESE PIE

Crisco pastry for 1-crust pie
2 cups (8 ounces) shredded
   cheddar cheese
1/4 cup finely chopped onion
1 1/2 cups diced cooked ham
1/3 cup flour
1/2 teaspoon salt
1/4 teaspoon pepper
1/4 teaspoon caraway seed
1 cup milk
4 eggs

Line 9-inch pie plate with pastry; flute edges. Sprinkle half the cheese in pastry shell; top with half the onion and then half the ham. Repeat layers. In bowl, combine flour, salt, pepper, and caraway; gradually blend in milk. Add eggs, one at a time; beat well after each addition. Pour over pie. Bake at 350° for 55 to 65 minutes. Makes 6 to 8 servings.

## PORK CHOPS WITH SAFFRON RICE

6 pork chops, cut 1/2- to
   3/4-inch thick
1/2 teaspoon salt
Dash pepper
2 tablespoons Crisco
1 package (6 ounces) saffron
   rice mix or 2/3 cup long-
   grain rice
1/2 cup chopped onion
1 beef bouillon cube
1 3/4 cups hot water
1/2 cup dairy sour cream

Sprinkle chops with the salt and pepper. In large skillet, slowly brown chops in hot Crisco; drain off excess fat. Add rice mix and onion. Dissolve bouillon cube in hot water; pour over rice. Bring to boiling; reduce heat. Cover and cook over low heat for 40 minutes, until chops are tender; stir occasionally. Add an additional 1/2 cup water during cooking, if needed. Remove chops to warmed platter; stir sour cream into rice mixture. Cook and stir over low heat just until heated through. Makes 6 servings.

## PORK APPLE DINNER

1 1/2 pounds lean pork, cut
   in 1-inch cubes (3 1/2 cups)
3 tablespoons Crisco
1 cup water
1/2 cup chopped onion
1 teaspoon ground sage
3/4 teaspoon salt
1/2 cup milk
1/4 cup flour
3 cups thinly sliced, pared,
   cored cooking apples
   (2 large apples)
1 tablespoon sugar

In 3-quart saucepan, brown pork cubes in hot Crisco over medium-high heat. Add water, onion, sage, and salt; cover and simmer 20 minutes or until meat is tender. Combine milk and flour; stir into pork mixture. Cook and stir until mixture is thickened and bubbly. Turn half the hot pork mixture into 2-quart casserole. Place apple slices over meat; sprinkle with sugar and top with remaining pork mixture. Bake at 450° for 10 minutes; reduce heat to 350° and bake an additional 25 minutes. Makes 6 servings.

*Cut tenderized pork cutlets into strips, then stir-fry with vegetables for Oriental Skillet Supper. Serve this super-quick dish on gingered rice.*

# BUDGET STRETCHERS

**Balancing a food budget can be a challenge these days. Start by planning your meals using these appealing recipes. Then shop with a shrewd eye for bargains, and cook with a minimum of waste—you can't lose.**

## BEST EVER FRIED CHICKEN

3/4 cup flour
1 teaspoon salt
1/4 teaspoon pepper
1 frying chicken (2 1/2 to 3 pounds), cut up
2/3 cup Crisco

In paper or plastic bag, combine flour, salt, and pepper; add chicken, a few pieces at a time; shake to coat. Preheat Crisco in electric skillet to 360°, or use medium-high heat of range. Fry chicken for 30 to 40 minutes, uncovered, without lowering the heat. Turn chicken 4 to 5 times during frying for even browning. Makes 4 servings.

## BARBECUED FRIED CHICKEN

1/3 cup flour
1 teaspoon salt
1 frying chicken (2 1/2 to 3 pounds), cut up
3 to 4 tablespoons Crisco
1 cup catsup
1/2 cup water
1/2 cup chopped onion
1 small clove garlic, minced
1 teaspoon salt
1/4 teaspoon pepper
3 tablespoons lemon juice

In paper or plastic bag, combine flour and the first 1 teaspoon salt. Add chicken pieces, a few at a time; shake to coat. In large skillet, brown chicken in hot Crisco. Meanwhile, in saucepan, combine catsup, water, onion, garlic, the remaining 1 teaspoon salt, and the pepper. Heat to boiling; reduce the heat and simmer, uncovered, for 20 minutes. Remove from heat and add lemon juice; mix well. When chicken is browned, add sauce to chicken; cover and cook slowly for 35 to 40 minutes or until tender. Turn chicken frequently during cooking. Makes 4 servings.

## FRIED FISH

1/4 cup flour
1 teaspoon salt
1 egg
2 tablespoons water
4 fish fillets or steaks
1/2 cup fine dry bread crumbs
1/2 cup Crisco

In shallow bowl, combine flour and salt. In another bowl, combine egg and water. Dip fish in flour mixture, then in egg mixture, and finally in crumbs. In skillet, fry fish in hot Crisco on both sides until tender and golden, 20 minutes. Makes 4 servings.

## FISH & CHIPS

1 pound fresh or frozen fish fillets
1 pound potatoes, peeled (3 potatoes)
Crisco for deep frying
1/4 cup flour
1/2 teaspoon salt
1 egg yolk
2 tablespoons water
1 tablespoon Crisco, melted
1 egg white, stiffly beaten
1/4 cup flour

Thaw frozen fish. Cut into serving-size pieces. Cut potatoes in uniform strips, slightly larger than for French fries. To make chips: Fry potato strips in deep Crisco heated to 375° until golden brown, about 7 to 8 minutes. Remove, drain, and keep warm. In medium bowl, combine the first 1/4 cup flour and the salt. Make well in center; add egg yolk, water, and melted Crisco. Stir until batter is smooth. Fold in egg white. Dip fish in the remaining 1/4 cup flour, then into batter. Fry fish in deep Crisco heated to 375° until golden brown, about 1 1/2 minutes on each side. Sprinkle fish and chips with salt. To serve, sprinkle fish with vinegar, if desired. Makes 3 to 4 servings.

*When it comes to family-size savings, chicken is a winner. Our Best Ever Fried Chicken is guaranteed to please your family and your pocketbook, too.*

## DEEP FRIED CHICKEN

1 frying chicken (2 1/2 to
   3 pounds), cut up
1 cup water
1 egg
3/4 cup milk
3 tablespoons Crisco, melted
1 cup sifted flour
1/4 teaspoon salt
Crisco for deep frying

In a heavy pan with tight cover, place chicken on a rack; add the water and bring to boiling. Reduce heat, cover and steam for 20 minutes, until tender. Drain. In bowl, combine egg and milk; add melted Crisco. Stir in flour and salt; beat until smooth. Dip chicken pieces in batter; drain well on rack over waxed paper. Place a few pieces of chicken in wire basket; lower into deep Crisco heated to 375°. Fry about 4 minutes or until golden. Drain on paper toweling. Repeat until all chicken is cooked. Makes 4 servings.

## MARYLAND FRIED CHICKEN

3/4 cup flour
1 teaspoon salt
1/4 teaspoon pepper
2 frying chickens (2 1/2 to
   3 pounds each), cut up
2 eggs, beaten
1/2 cup Crisco

In bowl, combine flour, salt, and pepper. Dip chicken pieces first in beaten egg, then in flour mixture to coat. Brown chicken in hot Crisco. Reduce heat. Cover and cook until tender, 30 to 40 minutes. Serve with White Sauce, page 85. Makes 6 to 8 servings.

## HERB FRIED CHICKEN

1/3 cup flour
1 teaspoon salt
1/2 teaspoon dried thyme
1/2 teaspoon dried marjoram
1/2 teaspoon celery salt
1/4 teaspoon pepper
1 frying chicken (2 1/2 to
   3 pounds), cut up
2/3 cup Crisco

In paper or plastic bag, combine flour, salt, thyme, marjoram, celery salt, and pepper. Add chicken pieces, a few at a time; shake to coat. Preheat Crisco in electric skillet to 360°, or use medium-high heat of range. Fry chicken for 30 to 40 minutes, uncovered, without lowering heat. Turn the chicken pieces 4 to 5 times during frying for even browning. Makes 4 servings.

## MEXICANA CHICKEN

1/2 cup flour
2 teaspoons salt
2 teaspoons paprika
1/2 teaspoon pepper
1 frying chicken (2 1/2 to
   3 pounds), cut up
1/4 cup Crisco
1 can (10 ounces) condensed
   cream of tomato soup
1 can (3 ounces) sliced
   mushrooms, drained
1/2 teaspoon garlic salt
1/2 teaspoon chili powder
Dash dried basil
1 medium onion, thinly sliced

In paper or plastic bag, combine flour, salt, paprika, and pepper. Add 2 to 3 pieces of chicken at a time to bag and shake to coat. In large skillet, brown chicken on all sides in hot Crisco. Meanwhile, in small bowl, combine tomato soup, mushrooms, garlic salt, chili powder, and basil. After chicken is browned, remove to shallow baking dish. In same skillet, cook onion until tender. Top chicken with onion and tomato soup mixture. Cover and bake at 350° for 45 minutes. Remove cover and bake 15 minutes more or until chicken is tender. Makes 4 to 6 servings.

## CHICKEN CHEESE BAKE

1 frying chicken (2 1/2 to
   3 pounds), cut up
1 cup cracker crumbs
1/2 cup Crisco
1 can (10 3/4 ounces)
   condensed cheddar cheese
   soup
1/2 envelope (3 tablespoons)
   dry onion soup mix
1/2 cup milk

Coat chicken pieces with cracker crumbs. In large skillet, brown chicken in hot Crisco. Remove chicken to 2-quart casserole or baking dish. Combine cheese soup, onion soup mix, and milk; pour over chicken. Sprinkle any remaining cracker crumbs over the top. Bake at 350° for 50 to 60 minutes, or until chicken is tender. Makes 4 to 6 servings.

Lemon Chicken is not only a thrifty treat, but it's also easy on the cook. It uses just one skillet from start to finish. Serve with thick red tomato slices and hot fluffy rice.

## LEMON CHICKEN

1/3 cup flour
1 teaspoon salt
1 teaspoon paprika
1 frying chicken (2 1/2 to 3 pounds), cut up
3 tablespoons lemon juice
3 tablespoons Crisco
1 chicken bouillon cube
1/4 cup sliced green onion
2 tablespoons brown sugar
1 1/2 teaspoons grated lemon peel

In paper or plastic bag, combine flour, salt, and paprika. Brush chicken with lemon juice. Add 2 to 3 pieces of chicken at a time to bag and shake well. In large skillet, brown chicken in hot Crisco. Dissolve bouillon cube in 3/4 cup boiling water; pour over chicken. Stir in onion, brown sugar, peel, and any remaining lemon juice. Cover; reduce heat. Cook chicken over low heat until tender, 40 to 45 minutes. Sprinkle with chopped parsley, if desired. Makes 4 servings.

## SOUTHERN CHICKEN PIES

8 ounces bulk pork sausage
1/4 cup Crisco
1/3 cup flour
1/4 teaspoon salt
1/8 teaspoon pepper
1 can (13 3/4 ounces) chicken broth
2/3 cup milk
2 cups cubed cooked chicken
1 package (10 ounces) frozen peas, thawed
1 1/3 cups sifted flour
1/2 teaspoon salt
1 teaspoon celery seed
1/2 teaspoon paprika
1/2 cup Crisco
3 tablespoons water

In saucepan, brown sausage; drain on paper toweling. Pour out fat. In same saucepan, melt the 1/4 cup Crisco. Blend in the 1/3 cup flour, the 1/4 teaspoon salt, and the pepper. Stir in chicken broth and milk. Cook and stir until thickened and bubbly; cook 1 minute more. Add chicken, sausage, and peas; heat through. Divide among six 1-cup casseroles. Top with **Savory Pastry**: Combine the 1 1/3 cups flour, the 1/2 teaspoon salt, the celery seed, and paprika. Cut in the 1/2 cup Crisco until mixture is uniform and resembles coarse crumbs. Sprinkle with water, a tablespoon at a time; mix with fork until all flour is moistened and dough clings together; press into ball. Roll 1/8 inch thick on floured surface. Cut in 6 circles the size of casseroles. Cut slits near center of each circle; place one on each casserole. Bake at 425° for 25 to 30 minutes. Makes 6 servings.

## OVEN SWISS STEAK

1 1/2 pounds boneless beef round steak, 3/4 inch thick
1/4 cup flour
1 teaspoon salt
3 tablespoons Crisco
1 can (16 ounces) stewed tomatoes
1/2 cup chopped celery
1/2 cup chopped carrot
2 tablespoons chopped onion
1/2 teaspoon worcestershire sauce
1/4 cup (1 ounce) shredded process American cheese

Cut meat in 4 portions. Combine flour and salt; pound into meat, reserving remaining flour for sauce. Brown meat in hot Crisco. Transfer meat to shallow baking dish. Blend reserved flour mixture into pan drippings in skillet. Add tomatoes, celery, carrot, onion, and worcestershire to drippings and cook; stir constantly until mixture boils. Pour over meat. Cover and bake at 350° for 2 hours or until meat and vegetables are tender. Sprinkle cheese over meat. Return to oven for a few minutes to melt cheese. Makes 4 servings.

## HAMBURGER POT PIE

1 recipe Crisco pastry for 2-crust pie
1 teaspoon onion salt
1 tablespoon Crisco
1 pound ground beef
1/2 cup chopped onion
1 can (16 ounces) green beans or 2 cups frozen green beans, thawed
1 can (10 ounces) condensed tomato soup
1 tablespoon sugar
1 teaspoon salt
1/4 teaspoon pepper
1/8 teaspoon dried oregano

Prepare Crisco pastry as directed except omit the salt and substitute 1 teaspoon onion salt. Line 9-inch pie plate with pastry. In skillet, heat Crisco. Add ground beef and onion; cook just until meat is browned. Stir in green beans, soup, and seasonings. Pour meat mixture into pastry. Place top crust over filling; cut slits for escape of steam. Seal and flute edge. Bake at 400° for 25 minutes.

## CHEESY POTATOES & FRANKS

1/2 cup chopped onion
1/4 cup Crisco
1/4 cup flour
1 teaspoon salt
2 cups milk
1 cup (4 ounces) shredded process American cheese
1 tablespoon prepared mustard
1/2 pound frankfurters
3 cups sliced potatoes

In saucepan, cook onion in hot Crisco until tender; stir in flour and salt. Add milk; cook and stir over low heat until thickened and bubbly. Remove from heat; stir in cheese and mustard. Cut frankfurters in 1/4-inch slices. In greased 2-quart casserole, arrange layers of half the potatoes, frankfurters, and cheese sauce; repeat layers. Bake at 325° for 1 1/4 hours. Makes 6 to 8 servings.

## CRANBERRY PORK CHOPS

8 pork rib chops, 3/4 inch thick
2 tablespoons Crisco
1 can (16 ounces) whole cranberry sauce
1/2 cup bottled barbecue sauce
1/4 cup water
2 tablespoons cornstarch
1/4 cup cold water
Hot cooked rice

In large skillet, brown chops in hot Crisco; season with salt and pepper. Drain off excess fat. Combine cranberry sauce, barbecue sauce, and the first 1/4 cup water; pour over chops. Cover and simmer until chops are tender, 45 to 55 minutes. Remove chops to warmed platter; keep hot. Combine cornstarch and the cold water; stir into sauce in skillet. Cook and stir until thickened and bubbly. Spoon some sauce over chops; pass additional sauce and serve with rice. Makes 8 servings.

*Tomato-sauced round steak is topped with golden shreds of sharp cheese for this Oven Swiss Steak. A crisp chilled green salad will round out this tasty menu.*

## CRUSTY WATER ROLLS

3 to 3 1/4 cups sifted flour
1 package active dry yeast
1 cup water
1 tablespoon sugar
2 tablespoons Crisco
1 1/2 teaspoons salt
2 egg whites

In large mixer bowl, combine 1 1/4 cups of the flour and the yeast. Heat together water, sugar, Crisco, and salt just until warm; stir occasionally to melt Crisco. Add to dry ingredients in mixer bowl; add egg whites. Beat at low speed of electric mixer for 1/2 minute; scrape sides of bowl constantly. Beat 3 minutes at high speed. By hand, stir in enough of the remaining flour to make a moderately soft dough. Turn dough out onto floured surface; knead 8 to 10 minutes. Place dough in greased bowl; turn once to grease surface. Cover; let rise in warm place until double, 50 to 60 minutes. Punch down dough; cover and let rest 10 minutes. Divide dough in 20 to 24 balls; make each into oval shape. Place rolls on greased baking sheet. With sharp knife, make 1/8-inch-deep lengthwise slit across top of each roll. Cover; let rise until double, 30 to 40 minutes. Place large shallow baking pan on bottom oven rack; fill pan with boiling water. Bake rolls on rack above water at 450° for 10 to 12 minutes, until golden. Makes 20 to 24 rolls.

*Budget tip: Make use of stale bread slices. Slowly oven-dry the slices, whole or cubed. Crush slices to make bread crumbs. The bread cubes, now croutons, are delicious in tossed salads.*

## CINNAMON SWIRL LOAF

7 to 7 1/2 cups sifted flour
1 package active dry yeast
2 cups milk
1/2 cup sugar
1/2 cup Crisco
1/4 cup water
2 teaspoons salt
2 eggs
3/4 cup sugar
1 1/2 tablespoons cinnamon
Softened butter or margarine

In large mixer bowl, combine 3 1/2 cups of the flour and the yeast. In saucepan, heat together milk, the 1/2 cup sugar, the Crisco, water, and salt just until warm; stir occasionally to melt Crisco. Add to dry ingredients in mixer bowl; add eggs. Beat at low speed of electric mixer for 1/2 minute; scrape sides of bowl constantly. Beat 3 minutes at high speed. By hand, stir in enough of the remaining flour to make a soft dough. Turn out on lightly floured surface; knead until smooth. Place in greased bowl; turn once to grease surface. Cover; let rise until double, 1 1/2 to 2 hours. Punch down; divide in half. Cover and let rest 10 minutes. Roll each half to 15x7-inch rectangle, about 1/2 inch thick. Combine the 3/4 cup sugar and the cinnamon. Brush entire surface of dough with water. Sprinkle with all but 2 tablespoons of the cinnamon-sugar mixture. Roll up jelly roll fashion, beginning with narrow side. Seal long edge. Place sealed edge down, in 2 greased 9x5x3-inch loaf pans. Let rise until almost double, 45 to 60 minutes. Just before baking, brush loaves with softened butter and sprinkle with the reserved cinnamon-sugar. Bake at 375° for 35 to 40 minutes or until done. If crust browns too quickly, cover with foil the last 15 to 20 minutes of baking. When cool, drizzle with Confectioners Sugar Glaze, page 27. Makes 2 loaves.

*Home-baked bread is a popular money-saver. Add dark swirls of sugar and spice, and presto—Cinnamon Swirl Loaf for supper. It makes great toast, too.*

# GRANDMA'S OATMEAL BREAD

5 1/2 to 5 3/4 cups flour
1 cup quick-cooking rolled oats
2 packages active dry yeast
1 3/4 cups water
1/2 cup light molasses
1/3 cup Crisco
1 tablespoon salt
2 eggs
1 egg white
1 tablespoon water

In large mixer bowl, combine 2 1/2 cups of the flour, the oats, and yeast. In saucepan, heat together the 1 3/4 cups water, the molasses, Crisco, and salt just until warm; stir occasionally to melt Crisco. Add to dry ingredients in mixer bowl; add eggs. Beat at low speed of electric mixer for 1/2 minute; scrape sides of bowl constantly. Beat 3 minutes at high speed. By hand, stir in enough of the remaining flour to make a soft dough. Turn dough out on lightly floured surface; cover and let rest 10 minutes. Knead dough until smooth. Place in lightly greased bowl; turn once to grease surface. Cover; let rise in warm place until double, about 1 1/2 hours. Punch down dough. Coat 2 well-greased 9x5x3-inch loaf pans with about 2 tablespoons rolled oats each. Divide dough in half. Shape dough in loaves; place in pans. Cover and let rise until double, 45 to 60 minutes. Combine egg white and the remaining water; brush over tops of loaves. Sprinkle lightly with rolled oats. Bake at 375° for 40 minutes. Cover loosely with foil last 20 minutes of baking if crusts brown too quickly. Makes 2 loaves.

*Outdoors at the camp site or indoors at home, Pancakes are a sure winner with hungry families. Our hot-from-the-griddle cakes are sure to please the budget, as well.*

## PANCAKES

2 cups sifted flour
3 teaspoons baking powder
1 teaspoon salt
2 eggs
2 cups milk
1/4 cup Crisco, melted

In bowl, combine flour, baking powder, and salt. Combine eggs and milk; stir in melted Crisco. Add milk mixture to flour mixture; blend thoroughly. Pour batter on hot, greased griddle or in lightly greased skillet. Turn when tops are bubbly and edges browned. Makes 16 pancakes.

## HUSH PUPPIES

2 cups yellow cornmeal
1 tablespoon flour
1 teaspoon salt
1 teaspoon baking powder
1/2 teaspoon baking soda
3 tablespoons chopped onion
1 cup buttermilk
1 egg, beaten
Crisco for deep frying

In bowl, combine cornmeal, flour, salt, baking powder, and soda. Add onion, buttermilk, then egg; blend. Drop from tablespoon, a few at a time, into deep Crisco heated to 375°. Fry until golden. Drain on paper toweling. Makes 4 servings. If desired, Hush Puppies may be shallow fried.

## HAM FRITTERS

1 cup sifted flour
1 tablespoon sugar
1/2 teaspoon salt
1 teaspoon baking powder
1 egg
1/2 cup milk
1 cup chopped cooked ham
1 tablespoon Crisco, melted
Crisco for deep frying

In bowl, combine flour, sugar, salt, and baking powder. Combine egg and milk; add to dry ingredients. Stir in ham and melted Crisco. Drop from tablespoon, a few at a time, into deep Crisco heated to 375°. Fry until golden and cooked through, 3 to 5 minutes. Drain on paper toweling. Serve hot with Cheese Sauce, page 85. Makes 4 servings. If desired, fritters may be shallow fried.

## CORN FRITTERS

1 egg
1/2 cup milk
1 can (12 ounces) whole kernel corn
1 tablespoon Crisco, melted
1 cup sifted flour
1 tablespoon sugar
1/2 teaspoon salt
1 teaspoon baking powder
Crisco for deep frying

In bowl, combine egg and milk. Stir in corn and melted Crisco. Combine flour, sugar, salt, and baking powder; add to egg mixture; stir just to evenly distribute ingredients. Drop from tablespoon, a few at a time, into deep Crisco heated to 375°. Fry until golden and cooked through, 4 to 5 minutes. Drain on paper toweling. Serve hot with maple syrup. Makes 15 to 20 fritters. If desired, fritters may be shallow fried.

## QUICK SALMON PATTIES

1 can (16 ounces) pink salmon
1 egg
1/3 cup minced onion
1/2 cup flour
1 1/2 teaspoons baking powder
1 1/2 cups Crisco for shallow frying

Drain salmon; reserve 2 tablespoons liquid. In mixing bowl, combine salmon, egg, and onion; stir in flour. Combine baking powder and the reserved liquid; stir into salmon mixture. Form in small patties; shallow fry in hot Crisco until golden, about 5 minutes. Serve with tartar sauce. Makes 4 to 6 servings.

## EASY SKILLET FRENCH FRIES

1 pound (2 1/3 cups) Crisco
1 pound (3 medium or 2 large) baking potatoes
Salt

Pare potatoes and cut lengthwise in 3/8-to 1/2-inch strips. Let stand in bowl with cold water. In large, heavy skillet, preheat Crisco to 360°; (takes about 5 minutes when heat control is set as follows: moderately high on electric range, low flame on gas range, 360° on electric skillet). Rinse and drain potatoes; blot dry with paper toweling. Add to hot Crisco; do not adjust heat except if using gas range turn to medium high. Stir potatoes 3 to 5 times during frying. Fry 9 to 12 minutes or until light brown. Drain on paper toweling; salt to taste. Serve immediately. Makes 4 servings.

*Snack time is the best time to serve Applesauce Oatmeal Cookies. They're studded with dark, delicious raisins and are especially good with cold milk.*

## COOKIE MIX

6 cups sifted flour
1 tablespoon salt
1 pound (about 2 1/3 cups) Crisco

In large mixing bowl, combine flour and salt; cut in Crisco until mixture resembles coarse crumbs. Store in covered container such as an empty 3-pound Crisco can. No refrigeration is needed. Makes 7 to 8 cups.

## BROWNIES

Combine 1 1/2 cups Cookie Mix, 1 1/2 cups sugar, and 1/2 teaspoon baking powder. Add 3 eggs, 3 squares (1 ounce each) unsweetened chocolate, melted and cooled, and 1 teaspoon vanilla; stir vigorously. Add 1/2 cup chopped nuts; blend well. Pour into greased 9x9x2-inch baking pan. Bake at 375° for 25 to 30 minutes. Sprinkle with confectioners sugar. Cool.

## NUT PUFFS

Combine 2 cups Cookie Mix and 1/2 cup confectioners sugar. Add 1 teaspoon vanilla and 3/4 cup chopped pecans; blend well until dough will just hold together. Shape in 1-inch balls. Place 1 inch apart on ungreased cookie sheet. Bake at 375° for 12 to 15 minutes; do not brown. Roll in confectioners sugar while hot. Makes 3 dozen.

## EASY DATE NUT BARS

Combine 1/2 cup Cookie Mix, 1/2 cup brown sugar, and 1/4 teaspoon baking powder. Add 1 egg, 1 tablespoon milk, and 1 teaspoon vanilla; stir vigorously. Add 1 cup each chopped dates and nuts; blend. Pour into greased 8x8x2-inch baking pan. Bake at 375° for 20 to 25 minutes. Sprinkle with confectioners sugar. Cool. Cut in bars.

## MOLASSES CRISPS

Combine 2 cups Cookie Mix, 3/4 cup brown sugar, 1/4 cup flour, 1 1/2 teaspoons baking soda, 1 teaspoon cinnamon, 1/2 teaspoon ground cloves, and 1/2 teaspoon ginger. Add 1 egg and 3 tablespoons molasses; stir vigorously. Chill dough. Roll to 1/4-inch thickness on lightly floured surface. Cut in desired shapes with floured cookie cutters. Place on greased cookie sheets and bake at 375° for 8 to 10 minutes. Makes 3 to 4 dozen.

## SPICY HERMITS

1 cup brown sugar
1/2 cup Crisco
1 egg
2 tablespoons water
1 1/2 cups sifted flour
1 tablespoon instant coffee
1/2 teaspoon baking soda
1/4 teaspoon salt
1/2 teaspoon cinnamon
1/4 teaspoon nutmeg
1/4 teaspoon ground cloves
3/4 cup raisins
1/2 cup chopped walnuts

In mixer bowl, cream together sugar and Crisco. Add egg; beat well. Stir in water. Combine flour, instant coffee, soda, salt, and spices; add to creamed mixture. Stir in raisins and nuts. Drop from teaspoon 2 inches apart on greased cookie sheet. Bake at 375° for 10 minutes. Makes 3 1/2 dozen.

## APPLESAUCE OATMEAL COOKIES

1 cup brown sugar
1 cup Crisco
1/2 cup granulated sugar
2 eggs
1 teaspoon vanilla
3/4 cup applesauce
1 cup sifted flour
1 teaspoon salt
1 teaspoon cinnamon
1/2 teaspoon baking powder
1/2 teaspoon baking soda
4 cups quick-cooking rolled
  oats
1 1/2 cups raisins

In mixer bowl, cream together brown sugar, Crisco, and granulated sugar until light and fluffy; beat in eggs and vanilla. Add applesauce; mix well. Combine flour, salt, cinnamon, baking powder, and soda; add to applesauce mixture; blend thoroughly. Stir in oats and raisins. Drop from teaspoon on greased cookie sheet. Bake at 400° until golden brown, 12 to 15 minutes. Makes 7 dozen.

## CEREAL COOKIES

1 cup granulated sugar
1 cup brown sugar
1 cup Crisco
2 eggs
1 teaspoon vanilla
2 1/2 cups sifted flour
1 teaspoon cream of tartar
1 teaspoon baking soda
1/4 teaspoon salt
2 cups crisp rice cereal

In large mixer bowl, cream together sugars and Crisco. Add eggs and vanilla; beat well. Combine flour, cream of tartar, soda, and salt; add to creamed mixture and mix well. Stir in cereal. Drop from teaspoon on ungreased cookie sheet; bake at 375° for 10 minutes. Makes 6 dozen.

# MAKE AHEAD/BAKE AHEAD

**Invest in your future by doing your cooking chores ahead of time—in your spare moments, perhaps while the children are napping or in school. Then reap the benefits by enjoying some quiet unhurried minutes right before dinner.**

## OVEN BEEF STEW

2 tablespoons flour
1 1/2 teaspoons salt
Dash pepper
1 1/2 pounds beef chuck, cut in 1-inch cubes
2 tablespoons Crisco
2 cans (10 1/2 ounces each) condensed tomato soup
2 soup cans water (2 1/2 cups)
1 1/2 cups chopped onion
1/2 teaspoon dried basil
4 medium potatoes
4 medium carrots
1/2 cup dry red wine or water

*Advance preparation:* Combine flour, salt, and pepper; use to coat meat. In Dutch oven, brown meat in hot Crisco; add soup, water, onion, and basil. Cover and bake at 375° for 1 hour. Remove from oven and cool. Refrigerate overnight or until ready to use.
*Before serving:* About 1 1/2 hours before serving time, pare and cube potatoes and pare and cut carrots in 1-inch pieces; add to stew mixture with wine. Cover and bake at 375° for 1 hour or until tender. Makes 4 to 6 servings.

## ITALIAN BREAD STICKS

2 cups sifted flour
2 teaspoons baking powder
1 1/2 teaspoons salt
1/3 cup Crisco
3/4 cup milk
1 egg white, slightly beaten
Sesame seed

In bowl, combine flour, baking powder, and salt. Cut in Crisco until mixture resembles coarse crumbs. Add milk; stir just enough to hold dough together. On lightly floured surface, knead dough 15 to 20 times. Roll dough to 12x6-inch rectangle, 1/2 inch thick. Cut in 24 strips 1/2-inch wide. Roll into cylindrical sticks; place on greased baking sheet, 1 inch apart. Brush sticks with egg white; sprinkle with sesame seed, if desired. Bake at 425° for 15 to 20 minutes. Reheat to serve.

## SAUERBRATEN

2 cups water
1/2 cup dry red wine
1/2 cup red wine vinegar
1 onion, thinly sliced
4 whole cloves
4 whole peppercorns
2 bay leaves
2 1/2-pound beef rump roast
2 tablespoons Crisco
1/3 cup gingersnap crumbs (5 cookies)

*Advance preparation:* In saucepan, combine water, wine, vinegar, onion, cloves, peppercorns, and bay leaves. Bring to boiling; simmer 5 minutes. Cool. Place roast in large bowl; pour wine mixture over the top. Turn roast to coat all sides; cover bowl tightly and refrigerate 2 to 3 days; turn twice each day.
*Before serving:* Remove roast from marinade; pat dry with paper toweling. Strain marinade. In Dutch oven, brown the roast in hot Crisco; add marinade and simmer, covered, until meat is tender, 1 1/4 to 1 1/2 hours. Add more water, if needed. Remove roast to platter. Pour pan juices into large measuring cup; skim off fat; add enough water to measure 2 cups liquid. Return juices to Dutch oven; stir in gingersnap crumbs. Cook and stir until crumbs are dissolved and gravy thickens, 5 to 10 minutes. Makes 6 to 8 servings.

*Subtly seasoned Oven Beef Stew tastes like a French classic. Serve generous bowls of the piping hot brew with crisp homemade Italian Bread Sticks.*

*You can make spaghetti and meatballs hours or weeks in advance. Just cook the meatballs and tomato sauce and freeze them separately until needed. Then simply combine and heat to serve over the spaghetti.*

## MOCK LASAGNA

1 pound lean ground beef
1 medium onion, chopped
1/4 cup Crisco
5 ounces broad noodles
1 1/2 cups cream-style cottage cheese, small curd
1 package (3 ounces) cream cheese
1 can (8 ounces) tomato sauce
1 can (6 ounces) tomato paste
1 teaspoon salt
1/4 teaspoon pepper
1/4 teaspoon dried oregano

*Advance preparation:* In large skillet, brown ground beef and onion in hot Crisco. Cook noodles according to package directions; drain. In small bowl, cream together cottage cheese and cream cheese. Drain excess fat from beef mixture; stir in tomato sauce, tomato paste, and seasonings. In 2-quart casserole, place half the noodles; top with half the meat mixture and cheese mixture. Repeat layers; spread last layer of cheese to completely cover top. Refrigerate.
*Before serving:* Bake, uncovered, at 350° for 30 minutes or until heated through. Makes 4 to 6 servings.

## CHICKEN CROQUETTES

3 tablespoons Crisco
1/3 cup flour
1 teaspoon salt
1 cup milk
2 cups chopped cooked chicken
2 tablespoons chopped parsley
1 tablespoon minced onion
2 eggs
2 tablespoons lemon juice
1/3 cup fine dry bread crumbs
Crisco for deep frying

*Advance preparation:* In saucepan, melt Crisco; stir in flour and salt. Stir in milk. Cook and stir over low heat until mixture thickens and bubbles. Stir in chicken, parsley, and onion. Spread mixture in greased shallow baking pan. Chill thoroughly.
*Before serving:* Divide mixture in 8 portions; shape each in a log. Beat together eggs and lemon juice. Dip each log into egg mixture, then roll in crumbs. Fry croquettes in deep Crisco heated to 375° until golden brown, 3 to 5 minutes. Drain on paper toweling. Makes 4 servings.

## SPAGHETTI

1 1/2 cups chopped onion
3 small cloves garlic, minced
3 tablespoons Crisco
2 cans (29 ounces each)
   tomatoes, cut up
1 can (12 ounces) tomato paste
4 beef bouillon cubes
2 tablespoons sugar
2 teaspoons dried oregano
1 teaspoon basil
1/4 teaspoon pepper
3 bay leaves
Meatballs, recipe below
2 cans (6 ounces each) sliced
   mushrooms, drained
1 tablespoon grated parmesan
   cheese
2 pounds spaghetti, cooked and
   drained

*Advance preparation:* In Dutch oven, cook onion and garlic in hot Crisco until tender but not brown. Stir in tomatoes, tomato paste, bouillon cubes, sugar, seasonings, and 3 cups water. Bring to boiling; reduce heat and simmer, uncovered, for 2 hours; stir occasionally. Remove bay leaves. Prepare Meatballs. Refrigerate or freeze sauce and Meatballs separately.
*Before serving:* Thaw sauce and Meatballs if frozen; heat sauce to boiling. Add Meatballs, mushrooms, and cheese; simmer until thickened, 30 minutes. To serve, spoon over hot spaghetti. Serve with additional parmesan cheese. Makes 14 servings.

## MEATBALLS

3 eggs, beaten
3/4 cup milk
2 cups soft bread crumbs
1/2 cup grated parmesan
   cheese
1 teaspoon salt
2 pounds ground beef
1 pound Italian sausage

*Advance preparation:* In large bowl, combine eggs, milk, crumbs, cheese, and salt. Mix in beef and sausage. Shape in 42 medium-size balls. Bake in shallow baking pan at 375° for 30 to 35 minutes; drain. Cool and freeze, if desired.
*Before serving:* Thaw if frozen. Add to Spaghetti or reheat in oven to serve. Makes 42 meatballs.

## PAUPIETTES DE BOEUF

1 can (3 ounces) chopped
   mushrooms, drained
1 tablespoon chopped onion
1 tablespoon Crisco
1 tablespoon butter or
   margarine
2 1/2 cups soft bread crumbs
1/2 teaspoon parsley flakes
1/4 teaspoon dried thyme
1/4 teaspoon salt
1/8 teaspoon pepper
2 1/4 pounds beef round
   steak, 1/4-inch thick
1/4 cup Crisco
1 can (11 ounces) condensed
   golden mushroom soup
2 tablespoons red wine or water

*Advance preparation:* Brown mushrooms and onion in the 1 tablespoon hot Crisco and the butter. In bowl, combine crumbs, parsley, thyme, salt, and pepper; add mushroom mixture. Cut meat in 6 pieces. Divide stuffing mixture among pieces of meat. Wrap meat around stuffing, forming a roll; secure with wooden toothpick. Brown meat rolls on all sides in the remaining hot Crisco. Combine soup and wine. Place meat rolls in 1 1/2-quart casserole; pour on sauce. Cover and chill.
*Before serving:* Bake covered casserole at 350° for 1 1/4 hours. Spoon sauce in casserole over meat rolls; bake 15 minutes more. Serve with hot cooked rice or noodles. Makes 6 servings.

## CITY CHICKEN

2 pounds veal, cubed
2/3 cup finely crushed saltine
   cracker crumbs
1 teaspoon paprika
3/4 teaspoon poultry
   seasoning
1/2 teaspoon salt
1 egg, slightly beaten
2 tablespoons milk
3 tablespoons Crisco
1 chicken bouillon cube

*Advance preparation:* Thread veal cubes onto six 9-inch skewers. Combine crumbs, paprika, poultry seasoning, and salt. Combine egg and milk. Dip meat in egg mixture, then in crumbs. Chill until ready to use.
*Before serving:* In large skillet, brown meat slowly on all sides in hot Crisco. Dissolve bouillon cube in 1/2 cup boiling water. Place skewered meat in 13x9x2-inch baking pan; pour bouillon over the top. Cover and bake at 350° for 45 minutes. Uncover; bake 30 minutes more. Makes 6 servings.

## WAFFLES

2 1/4 cups sifted flour
1 1/2 tablespoons sugar
4 teaspoons baking powder
3/4 teaspoon salt
2 eggs, beaten
2 1/4 cups milk
1/2 cup Crisco, melted
2 tablespoons flaked coconut
1 tablespoon grated orange
  peel
1/4 cup diced unpared apple
1 teaspoon sugar
Several dashes nutmeg
1/4 cup chopped pecans

*Advance preparation:* In bowl, combine flour, the 1 1/2 tablespoons sugar, the baking powder, and salt. Combine eggs, milk, and melted Crisco; stir into flour mixture just until dry ingredients are moistened. (Batter is thin.) In bowl, combine coconut and orange peel; in another bowl, combine apple, the remaining 1 teaspoon sugar, and the nutmeg. Pour batter onto preheated, preseasoned* waffle baker just until grid surface is 2/3 covered. Quickly top waffle batter with small amount of the coconut mixture, apple mixture, or the pecans, or bake waffles plain. Waffles are done when the steam stops and lid lifts easily. Wrap and freeze, if desired. Makes 1 dozen.
*Before serving:* Remove waffles from freezer; bake immediately at 325° for 15 minutes or heat in toaster. Serve with butter and syrup.
*Waffle iron should be preseasoned according to manufacturer's directions. Once conditioned, no greasing is necessary.

## APPLE NUT COFFEE CAKE

1/4 cup Crisco
1/2 cup granulated sugar
1 egg
1/2 teaspoon vanilla
1 cup sifted flour
1 teaspoon baking powder
1/4 teaspoon baking soda
1/8 teaspoon salt
1/2 cup dairy sour cream
3/4 cup finely chopped pared
  apple
1/4 cup chopped nuts
1/4 cup brown sugar
1/2 teaspoon cinnamon
1 tablespoon butter or
  margarine, melted

*Advance preparation:* In mixing bowl, cream Crisco and granulated sugar. Add egg and vanilla; beat well. Combine flour, baking powder, soda, and salt; add to creamed mixture alternately with sour cream. Fold in apple. Spread batter in greased 8x8x2-inch baking pan. Combine nuts, brown sugar, cinnamon, and butter. Sprinkle over batter. Bake at 350° for 30 to 35 minutes. Cool 10 minutes; remove from pan and serve. Or, cool thoroughly. Wrap coffee cake in foil and freeze.
*Before serving:* Heat frozen coffee cake in the foil wrap at 350° for 30 minutes or until heated through. Open foil during last 10 minutes.

## BROWN & SERVE ROLLS

3 1/2 cups sifted flour
1 package active dry yeast
1 1/4 cups milk
1/4 cup sugar
1/4 cup Crisco
1 teaspoon salt
1 egg

*Advance preparation:* In large mixer bowl, combine 2 cups of the flour and the yeast. In saucepan, heat milk, sugar, Crisco, and salt just until warm; stir occasionally to melt Crisco. Add to dry ingredients in mixer bowl; add egg. Beat at low speed with electric mixer for 1/2 minute; scrape sides of bowl constantly. Beat 3 minutes at high speed. By hand, stir in enough of the remaining flour to make a soft dough. Place dough in greased bowl; turn once to grease surface. Cover and let rise until double, 1 1/2 to 2 hours. Turn onto lightly floured surface; shape in rolls (see page 33). Place on greased baking sheet or in muffin pans. Cover; let rise until double, 30 to 45 minutes. Bake at 325° for 15 minutes; do not brown. Remove from pan; cool. Wrap in foil and freeze.
*Before serving:* Thaw rolls in the foil at room temperature 10 to 15 minutes. Unwrap; bake at 450° until golden brown, 5 to 10 minutes. Makes 24 rolls.

Next time you make Waffles, make a double
batch! Add chopped apple, coconut, or nuts
to those you serve now, then bake the
remainder plain and freeze them for later.

*Guests coming tomorrow?
Refrigerate dough for
Orange Crescents tonight.
These rolls will be ready
to rise and bake in the
morning, just in time for
your company brunch or
luncheon.*

*Your homemade rolls and breads will stay fresh
and moist after baking when wrapped tightly in
foil, or plastic wrap or bags. Store in a cool dry
place — don't refrigerate or you'll hasten staling.*

# ORANGE
# CRESCENTS

3 cups sifted flour
1 package active dry yeast
3/4 cup milk
1/4 cup water
1/4 cup sugar
1/4 cup Crisco
1 teaspoon salt
1 egg
1 teaspoon grated orange peel

*Advance preparation:* In mixer bowl, combine
1 3/4 cups of the flour and the yeast. In saucepan, heat together milk, water, sugar, Crisco, and
salt just until warm; stir occasionally to melt
Crisco. Add to dry mixture in mixer bowl; add egg
and orange peel. Beat at low speed of electric
mixer for 1/2 minute; scrape sides of bowl constantly. Beat 3 minutes at high speed. By hand, stir
in the remaining flour; mix well. Place dough in
greased bowl; turn to grease surface. Cover; refrigerate 2 to 24 hours.
*Before serving:* About 2 hours before serving,
remove dough from refrigerator and divide in
half. Roll each to 9-inch circle; cut each in 12
wedges. Starting at wide end, roll up each wedge.
Place points down on greased baking sheet. Let
rise in warm place until double, about 1 1/4 hours.
Bake at 375° for 10 to 12 minutes. While warm,
spread with **Orange Glaze:** Combine 1 1/2 cups
confectioners sugar, 1/2 teaspoon grated orange
peel, and enough orange juice to make desired
consistency. Makes 24 rolls.

## REFRIGERATOR HERB ROLLS

3 1/4 to 3 1/2 cups sifted
  flour
1 package active dry yeast
2 teaspoons celery seed
1 teaspoon dried thyme
1 1/4 cups milk
1/4 cup sugar
1/4 cup Crisco
1 teaspoon salt
1 egg

*Advance preparation:* In mixer bowl, combine 1 1/2 cups of the flour, the yeast, celery seed, and thyme. Heat together milk, sugar, Crisco, and salt just until warm; stir occasionally to melt Crisco. Add to dry ingredients in bowl; add egg. Beat at low speed of electric mixer for 1/2 minute; scrape sides of bowl constantly. Beat 3 minutes at high speed. By hand, stir in enough of the remaining flour to make a moderately soft dough. Place in greased bowl; turn once. Cover and chill.

*Before serving:* About 2 hours before serving, shape dough in 1 1/4 inch balls. Place 3 balls in each greased muffin pan to form 18 cloverleaf rolls. Brush with melted butter. Let rise until double, about 1 hour. Bake at 400° for 12 to 15 minutes. Makes 18 rolls.

## RAISIN SPICE MUFFINS

2/3 cup Crisco
1/2 cup sugar
2 eggs
1/2 cup sour milk
1/2 cup light molasses
2 cups sifted flour
1 teaspoon baking soda
1/2 teaspoon salt
1/2 teaspoon cinnamon
1/4 teaspoon ground cloves
1/8 teaspoon nutmeg
1 cup raisins

*Advance preparation:* Cream Crisco and sugar. Beat in eggs, milk, and molasses. Combine flour, soda, salt, and spices; stir into molasses mixture. Fold in raisins. Store in casserole with tight-fitting lid. Batter may be refrigerated, covered, up to 10 days.

*Before serving:* Without stirring batter, fill greased muffin pans 2/3 full. Bake at 350° for 25 to 30 minutes. Makes 18 to 20 muffins.

## ROYAL RYE ROLLS

4 cups stirred rye flour
2 packages active dry yeast
2 tablespoons caraway seed
2 1/4 cups milk
1/2 cup sugar
3 tablespoons Crisco
1 tablespoon salt
2 eggs
3 cups sifted all-purpose
  flour

*Advance preparation:* In mixer bowl, combine 3 1/2 cups of the rye flour, the yeast, and caraway seed. In saucepan, heat together milk, sugar, Crisco, and salt just until warm; stir occasionally to melt Crisco. Add to dry ingredients in mixer bowl; add eggs. Beat at low speed of electric mixer for 1/2 minute; scrape sides of bowl constantly. Beat 3 minutes at high speed. By hand, stir in the remaining rye flour and enough of the all-purpose flour to make a soft dough. Place in greased bowl; turn once. Cover and chill.

*Before serving:* Shape dough in 24 oval rolls. Let rise on greased baking sheet in warm place until double, about 1 hour. Brush with water; sprinkle with coarse salt and more caraway, if desired. Bake at 375° for 20 to 25 minutes or until done. Makes 24 rolls.

## SOUR CREAM COFFEE CAKE

1/2 cup Crisco
1 cup granulated sugar
2 eggs
1 cup dairy sour cream
2 cups sifted flour
1 1/2 teaspoons baking powder
1 teaspoon baking soda
1/4 teaspoon salt
1 cup chopped pecans
1/2 cup brown sugar
1/2 teaspoon cinnamon
1/2 cup dark raisins

*Advance preparation:* In mixer bowl, cream Crisco, granulated sugar, and eggs. Blend in sour cream. Sift together flour, baking powder, soda, and salt; add to creamed mixture; beat well. Combine nuts, brown sugar, and cinnamon. Spread half the batter in greased 10-inch tube pan. Sprinkle with raisins and half the nut mixture. Spoon on remaining batter. Top with remaining nut mixture. Bake at 350° for 45 to 50 minutes. Serve warm or cool; or wrap in foil and freeze.

*Before serving:* Heat frozen coffee cake in foil at 350° for 30 minutes. Open foil last 10 minutes.

Pies that wait in the freezer are worth their weight in gold to a busy home-maker. This frosty Fudge Ribbon Pie is topped with a fluffy peppermint meringue.

## FUDGE RIBBON PIE

1 Crisco pastry shell (9-inch)
1 quart pink peppermint ice cream, softened
1 tablespoon crushed peppermint stick candy
2 tablespoons butter or margarine
2 squares (1 ounce each) unsweetened chocolate
1 cup sugar
1 can (5 1/3 ounces) evaporated milk (2/3 cup)
1 teaspoon vanilla
3 egg whites
1/2 teaspoon vanilla
1/4 teaspoon cream of tartar
6 tablespoons sugar
3 tablespoons crushed peppermint stick candy

Bake and cool pastry. Spread 1 pint ice cream in bottom pastry shell; cover with half the Fudge Sauce. Freeze until firm. Repeat layers of ice cream and Fudge Sauce. Freeze until firm. Remove pie from freezer; spread Peppermint Meringue over chocolate layer. Seal meringue to edge of crust. Sprinkle with 1 tablespoon candy. Place pie on wooden board. Bake at 475° for 5 to 6 minutes, until meringue is golden.
**Fudge Sauce:** In saucepan, heat butter, chocolate, the 1 cup sugar, and the milk. Cook and stir over low heat until thick and bubbly. Add the 1 teaspoon vanilla; cool.
**Peppermint Meringue:** Beat egg whites with the remaining vanilla and the cream of tartar until soft peaks form. Gradually add remaining sugar; beat until stiff peaks form and all sugar is dissolved. Fold in the 3 tablespoons candy.

## ICE CREAM PIE

1 Crisco pastry shell (8- or 9-inch)
1 to 1 1/2 quarts ice cream, softened

Bake and cool pastry. Fill pastry shell with ice cream; spread evenly. Wrap in foil; fold edges under to seal. Freeze. Just before serving, top with fresh, frozen, or canned fruit and whipped cream.

## STRAWBERRY ICE CREAM PIE

Fill pastry shell with strawberry ice cream. Wrap in foil and freeze. Just before serving, top with fresh or partially thawed frozen strawberries. Spoon on whipped cream, if desired.

## PARTY PUMPKIN PIE

1 Crisco pastry shell (9-inch)
1 pint vanilla ice cream, softened
1 tablespoon chopped candied ginger
1 cup canned pumpkin
1/2 cup sugar
1/2 teaspoon salt
1/2 teaspoon ground ginger
1/4 teaspoon nutmeg
1 cup whipping cream
1 1/2 cups tiny marshmallows

Bake and cool pastry. Combine ice cream and candied ginger. Spread ice cream mixture in pastry shell. Freeze. In medium bowl, combine pumpkin, sugar, salt, ground ginger, and nutmeg. Whip cream; fold into pumpkin mixture. Add marshmallows. Spread pumpkin mixture over ice cream layer; freeze. Garnish with additional whipped cream, if desired.

## BANANA SPLIT PIE

1 Crisco pastry shell (9-inch)
3 medium bananas
1 tablespoon lemon juice
1 pint strawberry ice cream, softened
1 cup frozen whipped dessert topping, thawed
Whole maraschino cherries
2 tablespoons finely chopped walnuts
Chocolate sauce or Quick Fudge Sauce

Bake and cool pastry. Thinly slice bananas; sprinkle with lemon juice and arrange on bottom of pastry shell. Spread ice cream over bananas. Freeze until firm. Spread dessert topping over ice cream. Top with cherries; sprinkle with nuts. Freeze again until firm. Serve with canned chocolate sauce or prepare **Quick Fudge Sauce:** In saucepan, combine 1 package (6 ounces) semisweet chocolate chips (1 cup) and 1 can (5 1/3 ounces) evaporated milk (2/3 cup). Cook and stir over low heat until well combined. Beat in 1/2 pint marshmallow creme until mixture is thoroughly blended. Serve warm or cool.

King Kamehameha, Hawaii's last king,
would have loved this Hawaiian Pie. Top
it with toasted almond slices if macadamia
nuts aren't readily available.

## HAWAIIAN PIE

1 Crisco pastry shell (9-inch)
1 can (12 ounces) unsweetened
   pineapple juice
3/4 cup sugar
7 medium cooking apples,
   pared, cored and cut in
   wedges
3 tablespoons cornstarch
1 tablespoon butter or
   margarine
1/2 teaspoon vanilla
1/4 teaspoon salt

Bake and cool pastry shell. In large saucepan, combine 1 1/4 cups of the pineapple juice and the sugar. Bring to boiling; add apple wedges. Simmer, covered, until tender but not soft, 3 to 4 minutes. Lift apples from syrup; set aside to drain. Combine cornstarch and the remaining pineapple juice; add to syrup in saucepan. Cook and stir until thickened and bubbly; cook 1 minute more. Remove from heat; add butter, vanilla, and salt. Cool 10 minutes without stirring. Pour half the pineapple mixture into pastry shell; spread to cover bottom. Arrange cooked apples atop; spoon remaining sauce over. Chill. Garnish with whipped cream. Sprinkle with chopped macadamia nuts.

## FRENCH LEMON PIE

Crisco pastry for 1-crust pie
4 eggs
1 cup light corn syrup
1 teaspoon grated lemon peel
1/3 cup lemon juice
2 tablespoons butter or
   margarine, melted
1/2 cup sugar
2 tablespoons flour

Line 9-inch pie plate with pastry; flute edge. In medium bowl, beat eggs well; add corn syrup, lemon peel, lemon juice, and melted butter. Combine sugar and flour; stir into egg mixture. Pour into pastry shell. Bake at 350° for 50 minutes. Chill. To serve, top with dollops of whipped cream, if desired.

## BANANA RUM PIE

1 recipe Crisco pastry for
   1-crust pie
3 tablespoons finely chopped
   pecans
1 package vanilla pudding mix
   (4-serving size)
1 envelope (1 tablespoon)
   unflavored gelatin
2 1/4 cups milk
1 package fluffy white
   frosting mix
1 1/2 teaspoons rum flavoring
Dash each salt and nutmeg
3 bananas
1 square (1 ounce) semi-
   sweet chocolate
1 tablespoon butter or
   margarine

Prepare Crisco pastry as directed except add the pecans to dry ingredients before adding water. Line 9-inch pie plate; prick with fork. Bake and cool. In medium saucepan, combine pudding mix and gelatin. Cook according to directions on pudding package, using the 2 1/4 cups milk. Remove from heat; cover with waxed paper; set aside. Prepare frosting mix according to package directions. Stir in rum flavoring, salt, and nutmeg. Gradually fold hot pudding into frosting. Slice one banana into pastry shell; cover with half the filling. Repeat with second banana and remaining filling. Chill 3 to 4 hours. Diagonally slice remaining banana; arrange on pie. Melt together chocolate and butter; mix well. Drizzle over banana.

## SPICY COCONUT CHIFFON PIE

1 Crisco pastry shell (9-inch)
1 cup flaked coconut
1 teaspoon cinnamon
1/4 teaspoon ginger
1/8 teaspoon mace
1 envelope (1 tablespoon)
   unflavored gelatin
1/2 cup sugar
1/4 teaspoon salt
1 1/4 cups milk
4 egg yolks, beaten
1 teaspoon vanilla
1/4 teaspoon cream of tartar
4 egg whites
1/2 cup whipped cream

Bake and cool pastry shell. Combine coconut, cinnamon, ginger, and mace; spread in shallow pan. Toast at 350° for 8 minutes or until coconut is brown; stir occasionally. In medium saucepan, combine gelatin, sugar, and salt. Slowly stir in milk. Add egg yolks. Cook over low heat; stir constantly until mixture thickens; add vanilla. Cool thoroughly. In large mixer bowl, add cream of tartar to egg whites; beat until stiff but not dry. Whip cream. Fold egg whites and whipped cream into cooled egg yolk mixture. Chill until partially set. Pile half the chiffon mixture in pastry shell. Sprinkle half the coconut mixture over filling. Repeat layers; chill. Garnish with additional whipped cream.

# JUNIOR COOKERY

**Introduce the younger set to the rewards of home cooking arts with this collection of easy-to-make recipes. They're as fun to make as they are to eat, and your little chef may just decide to take over in the kitchen permanently!**

## PARTY DRUM CAKE

2 cups sifted flour
1 cup sugar
1 teaspoon baking soda
1 teaspoon salt
1 cup buttermilk or sour milk
1/2 cup Crisco
2 eggs
2 teaspoons vanilla
1 cup (6-ounce package) semi-sweet chocolate chips, melted and cooled

In large mixer bowl, combine dry ingredients. Add buttermilk, Crisco, eggs, and vanilla. Blend on low speed of electric mixer, then beat at medium speed for 2 minutes. Combine 1 cup batter and the melted chocolate. Pour light batter into 2 greased and floured 8x1 1/2-inch round layer cake pans. Spoon dark batter here and there over light batter. Make marble effect by pulling knife through batter in wide curves; turn pan and repeat. Bake at 350° for 30 to 35 minutes. Cool. Fill and frost with Fluffy Frosting, page 5. Decorate with small red gumdrops around bottom and top edges. Criss-cross red licorice strips on sides of cake. For drumsticks, cross 2 black licorice sticks on top; add a large red gumdrop to end of each.

## CHOCOLATE FUDGE CAKE

*This dark fudgy cake has its own built-in frosting. You sprinkle the batter with chocolate chips and walnut halves before baking. If you like, serve squares with scoops of chocolate chip ice cream.*

1/3 cup Crisco
1 cup sugar
1/2 teaspoon vanilla
2 squares (1 ounce each) unsweetened chocolate, melted and cooled
1 egg
1 1/4 cups sifted flour
1/2 teaspoon baking soda
1/2 teaspoon salt
3/4 cup water
1/2 cup semi-sweet chocolate chips
9 walnut halves

In large mixer bowl, cream Crisco and sugar until fluffy. Blend vanilla and chocolate into creamed mixture. Add egg; beat well. Sift together flour, soda, and salt; add to creamed mixture alternately with water; beat after each addition. Spread batter in greased and floured 9x9x2-inch baking pan. Sprinkle top of batter with chocolate chips; arrange nut halves over top. Bake at 350° for 30 minutes or until done. Cool in pan. Cut in squares.

## BROWN SUGAR CAKE

2 1/3 cups sifted cake flour
1 2/3 cups brown sugar
3 1/2 teaspoons baking powder
1 teaspoon salt
3/4 cup milk
2/3 cup Crisco
1/2 cup milk
3 eggs
1 teaspoon vanilla

In mixer bowl, combine flour, brown sugar, baking powder, salt, the 3/4 cup milk, and the Crisco. Beat vigorously by hand or at medium speed of electric mixer for 2 minutes. Add the 1/2 cup milk, the eggs, and vanilla; beat 2 minutes more. Pour batter into greased and floured 13x9x2-inch baking pan. Bake at 350° for 35 to 40 minutes. Cool on rack 15 minutes; remove from pan. Cool completely. Frost with Vanilla Frosting, page 27.

*This Party Drum Cake is chocolate marble inside and red rope licorice and gumdrops on the frosted outside. Let your children help decorate it for a birthday party.*

*Gingerbread Boys are perfect for snack time. If you like, bake wooden skewers into them and insert into shiny red apples to serve to the children.*

## GINGERBREAD BOYS

3 1/4 cups sifted flour
3/4 teaspoon salt
1 1/2 teaspoons baking powder
3/4 teaspoon baking soda
1 teaspoon ginger
1/4 teaspoon ground cloves
2 teaspoons cinnamon
1/2 teaspoon nutmeg
3/4 cup Crisco
3/4 cup sugar
3/4 cup molasses
1 egg

Sift together flour, salt, baking powder, soda, and spices. In large mixer bowl, cream together Crisco and sugar; add molasses and egg and beat well. Gradually add dry ingredients; stir to form a stiff dough. Chill 1 hour. On lightly floured surface, roll dough 1/4 inch thick. Cut in gingerbread boy shapes. Place 1 inch apart on greased cookie sheet. (To make cookies stand up, arrange bamboo skewers on baking sheet; place cookie on each, so skewer is 1/3 the way up back of cookie.) Decorate with red cinnamon candies for faces and buttons. Bake at 375° for 5 to 6 minutes. Cool slightly; remove from cookie sheet and cool on rack. Trim with Confectioners Sugar Glaze, page 27.

## SUGAR COOKIES

1 1/4 cups sugar
2/3 cup Crisco
2 eggs
1 tablespoon milk
1 teaspoon vanilla
3 cups sifted flour
2 teaspoons baking powder
1 teaspoon salt

Cream sugar, Crisco, eggs, milk, and vanilla. Combine flour, baking powder, and salt; blend into egg mixture. Roll 1 1/8 inch thick on lightly floured surface; cut with cookie cutter. Place on ungreased cookie sheet; bake at 375° for 8 to 10 minutes or until lightly browned. Remove from sheet immediately; sprinkle with sugar, if desired. Makes 6 to 7 dozen.

## SESAME FRIED CHICKEN

3/4 cup flour
1 teaspoon salt
1/4 teaspoon pepper
1 tablespoon sesame seed
1 frying chicken (2 1/2 to
   3 pounds), cut up
1/3 cup milk
2/3 cup Crisco

Combine flour, salt, pepper, and sesame seed. Dip chicken pieces in milk, then in seasoned flour to coat. In skillet, brown chicken on all sides in hot Crisco. Reduce heat; cover and cook until chicken is tender, 30 to 40 minutes. Makes 4 servings.

## FRANK-FRITTERS

1 tablespoon Crisco, melted
1 egg
1/2 cup milk
3/4 cup sifted flour
1/8 teaspoon red pepper
1/2 teaspoon dry mustard
1/2 teaspoon baking powder
1/2 teaspoon salt
12 frankfurters
Crisco for deep frying

Combine the melted Crisco, the egg, and milk. Combine dry ingredients; add to Crisco mixture and mix until smooth. Dip frankfurters in batter and fry until golden in deep Crisco heated to 375°. Makes 6 servings.

## BITE SIZE PIZZAS

Biscuit dough, page 30
Tomato sauce
Dried oregano
Grated cheese, mushrooms,
   sausage, or pepperoni

Prepare Biscuit dough as directed on page 30. Roll dough 1/4 inch thick; cut in 2-inch rounds. Place on baking sheet. Top with tomato sauce and oregano, then one or more of remaining ingredients. Bake at 425° for 10 to 12 minutes.

## BOLOGNA BASKETS

6 or 8 slices bologna
2 tablespoons Crisco
1 can (16 ounces) German-
   style potato salad

In stacks of 2 slices each, heat bologna in hot Crisco in skillet until meat forms cups. Heat potato salad in saucepan; fill meat cups with the salad. Makes 3 or 4 servings.

## REFRIGERATOR COOKIES

1 cup Crisco
2 cups brown sugar
2 eggs
3 1/2 cups sifted flour
1/4 teaspoon salt
1 teaspoon baking soda
1 teaspoon cream of tartar
1 cup chopped walnuts
1 teaspoon vanilla

Cream Crisco, sugar, and eggs. Mix dry ingredients and stir into creamed mixture. Add nuts and vanilla. Shape into 2 rolls and wrap in waxed paper or clear plastic wrap. Store in refrigerator until cold, about 6 hours. Slice 1/4 inch thick and place on ungreased cookie sheets. Bake at 375° for 5 minutes or until lightly browned. Makes 6 dozen.

## PEANUT BUTTER CHEWS

1/2 cup Crisco
1 cup brown sugar
1/2 cup peanut butter
1/2 teaspoon salt
1 egg
1 1/2 cups sifted flour
1 teaspoon baking soda

Cream together Crisco, brown sugar, peanut butter, salt, and egg. Combine dry ingredients and add to creamed mixture. Mix well; shape into 1-inch balls. Place 2 inches apart on ungreased cookie sheet. Flatten by pressing crisscross with tines of fork. Bake at 375° for 10 to 12 minutes. Makes 4 dozen.

## CHOCOLATE PEANUT PILLOWS

1 cup (6-ounce package)
   semi-sweet chocolate chips
1 tablespoon Crisco
1/2 cup peanut butter
2 tablespoons confectioners
   sugar
3 cups spoon-size shredded
   wheat biscuits
1/2 cup chopped peanuts

In medium saucepan, melt chocolate chips and Crisco over low heat. Remove from heat and stir in peanut butter and confectioners sugar. Dip biscuits in chocolate mixture; coat all sides; gently shake off excess. Roll the coated biscuits in peanuts. Cool on rack; store in refrigerator or very cool place. Makes 7 1/2 dozen.

# HOLIDAY SPECIALTIES

**Celebrate the special seasons with fresh-baked breads, doughnuts, pies, cakes, and cookies. Thanksgiving, Christmas, and Easter all seem merrier with bountiful baked treats to greet your guests.**

*If you make these Sugarplums before the holiday rush, you can freeze them, unfrosted, in moisture-vaporproof wrap for up to 3 months. Thaw wrapped loaves at room temperature, then frost.*

4 1/2 to 4 3/4 cups sifted flour
2 packages active dry yeast
1/4 teaspoon nutmeg
1 1/3 cups milk
1/2 cup sugar
1/4 cup Crisco
1 1/2 teaspoons salt
2 eggs
1/2 teaspoon vanilla
1 cup raisins
1/2 cup chopped mixed
   fruits and peels

## SUGARPLUM BREAD

In large mixer bowl, combine 2 3/4 cups of the flour, the yeast, and nutmeg. In saucepan, heat together milk, sugar, Crisco, and salt just until warm; stir to melt Crisco. Add to dry ingredients in mixer bowl; add eggs and vanilla. Beat at low speed of electric mixer for 1/2 minute; scrape sides of bowl constantly. Beat 3 minutes at high speed. By hand, stir in raisins, fruits, and enough of the remaining flour to make a soft dough. Turn out on lightly floured surface; knead until smooth. Place in greased bowl; turn once to grease surface. Cover; let rise until double, about 2 hours. Punch down. Divide dough in half. Cover and let rest 10 minutes. Shape half the dough into Baby Sugarplums; half into Little Sugarplum Loaves. Or shape into 2 Sugarplum Round Loaves.

## BABY SUGARPLUMS

Divide half the dough in 6 pieces. Shape each piece in 6 balls. Place in greased muffin pans. Cover and let rise until almost double, 45 to 60 minutes. Bake at 350° for 20 minutes. Drizzle each with Confectioners Sugar Glaze, page 27 and trim with walnut. Makes 3 dozen.

## LITTLE SUGARPLUM LOAVES

Divide half the dough in 4 pieces. Shape each into a loaf. Place in 4 greased 4 1/2x3x2-inch loaf pans. Cover and let rise until almost double. Bake at 350° for 20 to 25 minutes. Drizzle each with Confectioners Sugar Glaze, page 27 and trim with red and green candied cherries.

## SUGARPLUM ROUND LOAVES

Prepare Sugarplum Bread except substitute 1 teaspoon grated lemon peel for the vanilla and nutmeg. Let rise as above and divide in half. Shape each half into a ball. Place on greased baking sheets and pat tops to flatten slightly. Cover and let rise again until double, about 2 hours. Bake at 350° for 30 minutes. Drizzle with Confectioners Sugar Glaze, page 27 and trim with red candied cherries and slivers of green cherries.

*One basic Sugarplum Bread dough will make two Sugarplum Round Loaves. Next time make three dozen Baby Sugarplums plus four little loaves for holiday gifts.*

*Serve hot cider with a bounty of doughnuts: Raised Square Doughnuts, Cake Doughnuts, Country Style Doughnut Puffs, Fruited Doughnut Balls, Filled Doughnuts, and Crullers.*

# RAISED SQUARE DOUGHNUTS

3 1/2 to 4 cups sifted flour
2 packages active dry yeast
1 cup milk
1/3 cup sugar
1/3 cup Crisco
1 teaspoon salt
2 eggs
Crisco for deep frying

In large mixer bowl, combine 2 1/2 cups of the flour and the yeast. In saucepan, heat together milk, sugar, the 1/3 cup Crisco, and the salt just until warm; stir to melt Crisco. Add to dry ingredients; add eggs. Beat at low speed of electric mixer for 1/2 minute; scrape sides of bowl constantly. Beat at high speed 3 minutes. By hand, stir in enough of the remaining flour to make a moderately soft dough. Place in greased bowl; turn once to grease surface. Cover; chill 3 to 24 hours. Punch down. Turn out on lightly floured surface; roll 3/8 inch thick. Cut in squares. Place on greased baking sheet. Let rise until light, 30 to 40 minutes. Fry in deep Crisco heated to 375° for 1 1/2 minutes each side. Drain on paper toweling. While warm, roll in sugar.

# CAKE DOUGHNUTS

4 eggs
2/3 cup sugar
1/3 cup milk
1/3 cup Crisco, melted
3 1/2 cups sifted flour
3 teaspoons baking powder
1/2 teaspoon salt
1/4 teaspoon nutmeg
Crisco for deep frying

In mixing bowl, combine eggs and sugar. Stir in milk and the 1/3 cup Crisco. Combine flour, baking powder, salt, and nutmeg; beat into egg mixture until smooth. Chill dough about 2 hours. Roll on lightly floured surface to 3/8-inch thickness. Cut with floured doughnut cutter. Fry in deep Crisco heated to 375° until golden on both sides. Drain on paper toweling. While warm, roll in granulated sugar.

## COUNTRY STYLE DOUGHNUT PUFFS

2 eggs, beaten
1/2 teaspoon vanilla
1/2 cup sugar
1/2 cup milk
2 cups sifted flour
1 1/2 teaspoons baking powder
1/2 teaspoon salt
2 tablespoons butter or
  margarine, melted
Crisco for deep frying
1/2 cup sugar
1/4 teaspoon nutmeg

In medium bowl, combine eggs, vanilla, and the 1/2 cup sugar; beat well. Stir in milk. Combine flour, baking powder, and salt; stir into egg mixture until well mixed. Add melted butter. Drop batter from teaspoon into deep Crisco heated to 375°. Fry, a few at a time, until browned, 2 or 3 minutes. Drain on paper toweling. Combine remaining sugar and nutmeg; roll puffs in mixture to coat. Makes 3 to 3 1/2 dozen. For **Fruited Doughnut Balls,** stir 1/2 cup finely chopped pecans, 1/4 cup chopped raisins, 1/4 cup chopped dates, and 1 teaspoon grated orange peel into batter before frying.

## FILLED DOUGHNUTS

4 to 4 1/2 cups sifted flour
2 packages active dry yeast
1 1/4 cups milk
1/3 cup Crisco
1/4 cup sugar
1 teaspoon salt
2 eggs
18 prunes
1/4 cup sugar
Crisco for deep frying

In large mixer bowl, combine 2 1/2 cups of the flour and the yeast. In saucepan, heat together milk, the 1/3 cup Crisco, the first 1/4 cup sugar, and the salt just until warm; stir to melt Crisco. Add to dry ingredients; add eggs. Beat at low speed of electric mixer for 1/2 minute; scrape sides of bowl constantly. Beat at high speed 3 minutes. By hand, stir in enough of the remaining flour to make soft dough. Turn out on lightly floured surface and knead until smooth, 8 to 10 minutes. Place in greased bowl; turn once to grease surface. Cover; let rise until double, about 50 minutes. Meanwhile, cook prunes according to package directions, adding the remaining 1/4 cup sugar at beginning of cooking. Cool; halve and pit. Divide dough in half. Roll on lightly floured surface to 3/8-inch thickness. Cut with floured 2 1/2-inch cutter. Place prune half in center of each; fold dough over and seal edges. Repeat with remaining dough. Let rise until light, 20 minutes. Fry raised doughnuts in deep Crisco heated to 375° for about 1 minute on each side. Drain. Roll in sugar, if desired. Makes 3 dozen.

## CRULLERS

2 3/4 to 3 1/4 cups sifted flour
2 packages active dry yeast
1 cup milk
1/3 cup sugar
1/4 cup Crisco
1 1/2 teaspoons salt
1 egg
Crisco for deep frying

In large mixer bowl, combine 2 cups of the flour and the yeast. In saucepan, heat together milk, sugar, the 1/4 cup Crisco, and the salt just until warm; stir to melt Crisco. Add to dry ingredients; add egg. Beat at low speed of electric mixer for 1/2 minute; scrape sides of bowl constantly. Beat at high speed 3 minutes. By hand, stir in enough of the remaining flour to make a soft dough. Turn out on lightly floured surface. Knead until smooth, about 8 minutes. Place in greased bowl; turn once to grease surface. Cover and let rise until double, 1 to 1 1/2 hours. Punch down; let rise again until double. Punch down and let rest 10 minutes. On lightly floured surface, roll to 12x9-inch rectangle, 1/2 inch thick. Cut in half crosswise to make two 9x6-inch rectangles. Cut each half into twelve 9x1/2-inch strips. Roll each strip with hands to make rope; twist into cruller shape. Cover; let rise 45 minutes. Fry raised crullers in deep Crisco heated to 375° for about 2 minutes; turn once. Drain on paper toweling. Brush with Confectioners Sugar Glaze, page 27. Makes 2 dozen.

## CRANBERRY PEAR PIE

Crisco pastry for 2-crust pie
1/2 cup sugar
3 tablespoons flour
1/4 teaspoon cinnamon
1 tablespoon lemon juice
1 cup whole cranberry sauce
3 cups sliced fresh pears
1 tablespoon butter or
   margarine

Line 9-inch pie plate with pastry. Combine sugar, flour, and cinnamon. Blend with lemon juice and cranberry sauce. Fold in pears. Pour into pastry-lined pie plate; dot with butter. Place lattice crust over filling; seal and flute. Sprinkle top with additional sugar. Bake at 400° for 35 to 40 minutes.

## MINCEMEAT PIE

Crisco pastry for 2-crust pie
1 jar (28 ounces) prepared
   mincemeat
2 cups applesauce
2 tablespoons lemon juice

Line 9-inch pie plate with pastry. In bowl, stir together mincemeat, applesauce, and lemon juice. Pour into pastry-lined pie plate. Place top crust over filling; seal and flute. Cut slits for escape of steam. Bake at 400° for 40 minutes.

## PUMPKIN PIE

Crisco pastry for 1-crust pie
1/3 cup sugar
1 teaspoon salt
1 teaspoon cinnamon
3/4 teaspoon ginger
1/4 teaspoon ground cloves
1/4 teaspoon nutmeg
2 cups canned pumpkin
1/4 cup honey
1 cup evaporated milk
2 eggs

Line 9-inch pie plate with pastry. In bowl, combine sugar, salt, and spices. Stir in pumpkin and honey. In saucepan, heat milk; add with eggs to pumpkin mixture; blend thoroughly. Pour into pastry-lined pie plate. Bake at 425° for 10 minutes. Reduce temperature to 350°; bake 35 minutes more.

## PUMPKIN POUND CAKE

1 cup brown sugar
1 1/4 cups granulated sugar
1 1/4 cups Crisco
4 eggs
1 can (16 ounces) pumpkin
3 cups sifted flour
1 tablespoon salt
2 teaspoons baking soda
3 1/2 teaspoons cinnamon
1 teaspoon nutmeg
1/2 teaspoon allspice
1/2 teaspoon ginger
1/2 cup chopped pecans

In large mixing bowl, combine sugars, Crisco, and eggs; beat 2 minutes on medium speed of electric mixer; add pumpkin. Sift together flour, salt, soda, and spices; gradually blend into creamed mixture. Beat 2 minutes at high speed. Stir in nuts. Pour into greased and floured 10-inch tube pan. Bake at 350° for 60 to 65 minutes. Cool 15 minutes; remove from pan. To serve, top with whipped cream and **Butter Rum Sauce**: In saucepan, combine 1 cup granulated sugar and 2 tablespoons cornstarch. Add 1 1/3 cups water; cook and stir until thickened; cook 2 minutes more. Remove from heat; add 3 tablespoons rum (or 1 1/4 teaspoons rum flavoring) and 3 tablespoons butter.

## CRANBERRY NUT BREAD

1 1/2 cups cranberries
1/2 cup sugar
2 cups sifted flour
3/4 cup sugar
1 1/4 teaspoons baking powder
1/2 teaspoon salt
1/2 teaspoon baking soda
1 orange
1/4 cup Crisco
2 eggs
1/2 cup chopped nuts

In small saucepan, combine cranberries and the 1/2 cup sugar. Cook over medium heat until sauce bubbles, about 8 to 10 minutes; drain. Sift together flour, the remaining 3/4 cup sugar, the baking powder, salt, and soda. Grate peel of orange; squeeze juice into measuring cup. Add peel and enough water to make 3/4 cup liquid. Add mixture to dry ingredients with Crisco and eggs; mix well. Fold in nuts and drained cranberries. Pour into greased 9x5x3-inch loaf pan. Bake at 350° for 45 to 50 minutes. Cool. To serve, spread with softened cream cheese.

*Ring in the Thanksgiving and Christmas holidays with Cranberry Pear Pie. Under the lattice crust is a filling flavored with sliced pears and whole cranberry sauce.*

*Coffee Rum Pie could be the finale for your big holiday dinner; it's a cool chiffon pie, laced with light rum and topped lavishly with whipped cream and shavings of chocolate.*

## MOCK MINCE PIE

Crisco pastry for 2-crust pie
1 1/3 cups sugar
1/2 teaspoon salt
1/2 teaspoon cinnamon
1/4 teaspoon ground cloves
1/4 teaspoon ginger
1 1/2 cups minced pared
   apples
1 cup dark raisins
1/2 cup jellied cranberry sauce
1/3 cup chopped walnuts
1 teaspoon grated orange peel
1/2 teaspoon grated lemon peel
1/4 cup lemon juice
1 tablespoon butter or
   margarine

Line 9-inch pie plate with pastry. In bowl, combine sugar, salt, and spices. Add apple, raisins, cranberry sauce, nuts, orange and lemon peel, and lemon juice; mix well. Pour into pastry-lined pie plate; dot with butter. Place top crust over filling; seal and flute. Cut slits for escape of steam. Bake at 400° for 30 to 35 minutes. Serve warm topped with shredded cheddar cheese, if desired.

## CHRISTMAS TARTS

10 baked Crisco Tart Shells,
   page 102
1 can (16 ounces) lemon
   pudding
1 cup dairy sour cream
1 package (10 ounces) frozen
   raspberries, thawed
2 tablespoons sugar
1 tablespoon cornstarch

Prepare tart shells; cool. Stir together pudding and sour cream; chill. Drain raspberries, reserving 2/3 cup syrup. Mix sugar and cornstarch in small saucepan; gradually stir in reserved syrup. Cook and stir until mixture thickens and bubbles; remove from heat and chill. Fill tart shells with lemon mixture; top with a few raspberries. Spoon about 1 teaspoon raspberry glaze over each. Makes 10 servings.

## COFFEE RUM PIE

1 Crisco pastry shell (8-inch)
1 package vanilla whipped
   dessert mix (4 serving size)
2 teaspoons instant coffee
1/2 cup cold milk
1/3 cup water
3 tablespoons light rum or 1/2
   teaspoon rum extract
1/2 cup whipping cream

Bake and cool pastry. In small mixer bowl, combine dry dessert mix and coffee. Add milk and beat at high speed of electric mixer for 1 minute. Blend in the water and rum; beat at high speed 2 minutes more or until fluffy. Whip cream; carefully fold into mixture. Pile into pastry shell; chill 3 to 4 hours. Garnish each serving with additional whipped cream and shaved chocolate, if desired.

## HOLIDAY FRUIT CAKE

20 ounces mixed candied
   fruits
1 cup raisins
3/4 cup chopped dates
3/4 cup chopped nuts
1 1/4 cups flour
1/2 teaspoon salt
1/4 teaspoon baking soda
1/4 teaspoon baking powder
1/2 teaspoon each allspice,
   cinnamon, nutmeg, cloves,
   and mace
1/2 cup Crisco
1/2 cup brown sugar
2 eggs
1/4 cup sour milk
1/4 cup dark molasses

Mix fruits and nuts with 1/4 cup of the flour until well coated. Combine remaining flour, the salt, soda, baking powder, and spices. Cream Crisco and brown sugar; add eggs and beat thoroughly. Stir in dry ingredients alternately with milk and molasses; beat well. Fold in fruit mixture. Spread in greased and floured 9x5x3-inch loaf pan. Bake at 300° for 2 hours. If desired, decorate cooled loaf with cherries and pineapple.

## CANDIED FRUIT COOKIES

1 cup Crisco
2 cups brown sugar
2 eggs
1/2 cup buttermilk
3 1/2 cups sifted flour
1 teaspoon baking soda
1 1/2 cups each chopped
   candied fruit, dates, and nuts

Cream together Crisco and brown sugar. Stir in eggs and buttermilk. Combine flour and soda; stir into creamed mixture and beat well. Add fruits and nuts. Drop from teaspoon 2 inches apart on greased cookie sheet. Bake at 375° for 12 minutes. Makes 10 dozen cookies.

## DATE NUT LOAF

2 cups chopped dates
1 cup chopped walnuts
1/3 cup Crisco
3/4 cup brown sugar
1 teaspoon vanilla
1 egg
2 cups sifted flour
1 teaspoon baking powder
1 teaspoon baking soda
1 teaspoon salt

In large mixer bowl, combine dates, nuts, and Crisco. Pour in 1 cup boiling water; beat until Crisco breaks into small lumps. Cool to lukewarm, about 15 minutes. Add sugar, vanilla, and egg; mix well. Combine flour, baking powder, soda, and salt; add to date mixture and beat well. Pour into 9x5x3-inch loaf pan. Bake at 350° for 1 hour. Cool thoroughly before slicing.

## MINCE NUT BREAD

2 1/2 cups sifted flour
3/4 cup sugar
1/2 teaspoon baking soda
1/4 teaspoon salt
1 cup prepared mincemeat
1/2 cup Crisco, melted
1/4 cup molasses
1 egg, slightly beaten
1/2 cup chopped walnuts

In large mixer bowl, sift together flour, sugar, soda, and salt. In medium bowl, combine mincemeat, 1/2 cup water, the cooled Crisco, molasses, and egg. Add to dry ingredients; mix well. Stir in nuts. Turn into greased 9x5x3-inch loaf pan. Bake at 350° for 1 1/4 hours. Cool. Wrap and refrigerate overnight before serving.

## CHERRY COFFEE CAKE

2 1/4 to 2 1/2 cups sifted flour
2 packages active dry yeast
1/2 cup water
1/3 cup milk
1/4 cup sugar
1/4 cup Crisco
1 teaspoon salt
1 egg
1/2 cup raisins
1/4 cup candied cherries, cut up
2 tablespoons chopped candied citron

In large mixer bowl, combine 1 3/4 cups of the flour and the yeast. Heat together water, milk, sugar, Crisco, and salt just until warm; stir to melt Crisco. Add to dry ingredients in mixer bowl; add egg. Beat at low speed of electric mixer for 1/2 minute; scrape sides of bowl constantly. Beat 3 minutes at high speed. By hand, stir in raisins, cherries, citron, and enough of the remaining flour to make a soft dough. Turn out on lightly floured surface; knead until smooth, 5 to 8 minutes. Place in greased bowl; turn once to grease surface. Cover; let rise until double, 1 1/2 hours. Punch down; turn out on lightly floured surface. Cover and let rest 10 minutes. Shape according to pictured directions, opposite. Let rise until double, about 1 hour. Bake at 350° for 25 minutes. Drizzle with Confectioners Sugar Glaze, page 27. Top with halved candied cherries, if desired.

## EASTER COOKIES

2 cups Crisco
1 cup confectioners sugar (sift if lumpy)
2 teaspoons vanilla
4 1/2 cups flour
1 teaspoon salt

In large bowl, blend Crisco, sugar, and vanilla. Add flour and salt; mix until dough holds together. Shape as directed below; place on ungreased cookie sheet. Bake at 375° for 10 to 12 minutes. (Cookies brown on bottom only.) Cool on sheet for 10 minutes; remove and cool thoroughly. Frost with Confectioners Sugar Glaze, page 27, and decorate as desired. Makes 3 dozen.
**Easter Nests:** Shape dough into patties 2 inches across and 3/8 inch thick. Bake and cool. Spread with white glaze; pat green-tinted coconut around edges; put jelly beans in center.
**Easter Eggs:** Shape about 1 tablespoon dough around a nutmeat, date half, or chocolate bit. Form dough into egg shape. Bake and cool. Spread with pink or desired color glaze to cover egg completely. Decorate tops with bits of gumdrops, nuts, or sugar.
**Tinted Coconut:** Combine 1/2 teaspoon water and a few drops food coloring in a screw-top jar. Add coconut; cover and shake until evenly tinted.

## FASTNACHTS

1 cup milk
1 package active dry yeast
1 1/2 cups sifted flour
1/4 cup Crisco
1 teaspoon salt
1/4 cup sugar
1 egg
2 cups sifted flour
Crisco for deep frying

Heat milk slightly and add yeast to dissolve. Add the 1 1/2 cups flour and beat until smooth. Cover and let rise until double, 2 hours. Cream the 1/4 cup Crisco, salt, and sugar. Beat in egg; stir into yeast mixture. Add remaining 2 cups flour and mix thoroughly. Place in greased bowl; turn once to grease surface. Let rise again until double. Roll on lightly floured surface to 3/8-inch thickness. Cut with floured doughnut cutter. Let rise 45 minutes. Fry in deep Crisco heated to 375° for 3 to 5 minutes. Drain on paper toweling. While still warm, roll in additional sugar or glaze with Confectioners Sugar Glaze, page 27. Makes 18.

*Bake a touch of spring! Raisins, and candied cherries and citron grace this sunny Cherry Coffeecake, while halved cherries crown the top.*

To shape coffeecake: cut dough into 12 pieces; roll each between hands to form 8-inch ropes. Place 6 ropes, each curved in a horseshoe shape, around an imaginary 4-inch circle in center of baking sheet.

Form the remaining 6 ropes into doughnut shapes; join seamed ends at center of circle, allowing the rounded ends to overlap the first layer of horseshoe shapes at points in between the petals.

# COMPANY PLEASERS

**Whether you entertain formally or informally, have just a few friends over or a multitude, you'll find recipes here to help you entertain with ease. After all, a relaxed, confident hostess is the key to any successful party.**

## DIPPERS DRUMSTICKS

3/4 cup sifted flour
1 tablespoon salt
1 tablespoon paprika
1/4 teaspoon pepper
1 1/2 to 2 dozen small chicken drumsticks
Crisco for pan frying

In plastic or paper bag, combine flour, salt, paprika, and pepper. Add drumsticks, a few at a time, and shake to coat. Preheat Crisco (1/4 inch deep) in large skillet over medium-high heat. Place drumsticks in skillet; allow enough room for browning. (Use 2 skillets, if necessary.) Fry for 30 to 35 minutes or until tender; turn often to brown evenly. Serve with sauces below.
**Zippy Pineapple Sauce**: In saucepan, combine 1 jar (12 ounces) pineapple preserves, 1/4 cup each prepared mustard and horseradish; heat.
**Royal Red Sauce**: In saucepan, combine 1/2 cup extra-hot catsup and 6 tablespoons butter or margarine; heat just until blended.
**Creamy Dill Sauce**: Combine 1/2 cup sour cream, 1/4 cup mayonnaise, and 1/4 teaspoon dried dillweed. Let stand at room temperature 1 hour.

## FRIED DEVIL DOGS

1 egg
1/2 cup milk
1 tablespoon Crisco, melted
3/4 cup sifted flour
1/2 teaspoon salt
1/2 teaspoon baking powder
1/2 teaspoon dry mustard
1/8 teaspoon red pepper
6 to 8 frankfurters
1/4 cup fine dry bread crumbs
Crisco for deep frying

Beat egg slightly; add milk and melted Crisco. In mixing bowl, combine flour, salt, baking powder, and seasonings. Add egg mixture; beat well. Cut franks into 1-inch pieces. Dip in crumbs, then in batter. Fry in deep Crisco heated to 375° until browned. Drain on paper toweling.

## BELGIAN CHEESE CROQUETTES

4 tablespoons butter or margarine
1/3 cup flour
1 1/2 cups milk
Dash pepper
Dash nutmeg
3 egg yolks
4 cups (16 ounces) shredded natural Swiss cheese
2 eggs
1/2 cup milk
1/2 cup flour
1 cup fine dry bread crumbs
Crisco for deep frying

In medium saucepan, melt butter; blend in the 1/3 cup flour. Add the 1 1/2 cups milk all at once; cook and stir until thickened. Add pepper and nutmeg. Stir about 1/2 cup hot mixture into egg yolks; return to hot mixture. Cook and stir 10 minutes. Add cheese; stir until smooth. Spread cheese mixture in lightly greased 11x7x1 1/2-inch baking pan. Chill until firm. Cut chilled mixture into 12 portions. In small bowl, beat together the 2 eggs and the 1/2 cup milk. Roll cheese croquettes carefully in the 1/2 cup flour; dip in egg mixture, then roll in crumbs to coat. Fry in deep Crisco heated to 375° until golden, 2 to 3 minutes. Drain. Serve with Tomato Sauce, page 85.

*Crisp-crusted Dippers Drumsticks stand ready to meet hungry guests. Serve them as an appetizer or snack with several tasty sauces for dipping.*

*Perky pimiento stars cut with a knife or an hors d' oeuvres cutter decorate Quiche Wedges. This hot appetizer starts with a package of frozen rarebit to make it easy on the cook on a busy day.*

## QUICHE WEDGES

1 Crisco pastry shell (9-inch)
1 package (10 ounces) frozen Welsh rarebit
2 eggs
1/8 teaspoon pepper
5 slices bacon, crisp-cooked, drained, and crumbled
Pimiento strips cut into stars

Bake and cool pastry. Heat frozen rarebit at 350° for 10 to 15 minutes, until defrosted. Remove from oven; cool slightly. Beat eggs; add rarebit and pepper; mix until well blended. Stir in bacon; pour into pastry shell. Bake at 350° for 30 minutes or until knife inserted off center comes out clean. Cool 10 minutes; cut in wedges; top with pimiento. Makes 12 to 14 servings.

## PARTY CREAM PUFFS

1/4 cup Crisco
1/2 cup boiling water
1/2 cup sifted flour
1/4 teaspoon salt
2 eggs

In saucepan, combine Crisco and boiling water. Stir over low heat until Crisco is melted. Add flour and salt all at once and beat until completely smooth. Remove from heat. Add eggs, one at a time; beat vigorously after each. Drop from half-teaspoon on greased cookie sheet, 1 1/2 inches apart. Bake at 450° for 10 minutes; lower temperature to 350° and bake 10 minutes. Cool. Slice off tops; fill with desired filling. Serve as appetizer or dessert. Makes 40.

## EGG SALAD CANAPES

2 hard-cooked eggs, chopped
2 tablespoons finely chopped dill pickle
1 tablespoon mayonnaise
1/4 teaspoon salt
16 Canape Pastry Rounds

Combine eggs, pickle, mayonnaise, and salt; mix well and chill. To serve, spread on baked Canape Pastry Rounds. Makes 1 1/2 dozen.
**Canape Pastry Rounds:** Prepare Crisco pastry for 1-crust pie. Roll out on floured surface to 1/8-inch thickness. Cut into 2-inch rounds. Place on ungreased baking sheet; prick with fork. Bake at 425° for 10 to 12 minutes. Makes 4 dozen.

|  |  |  |
|---|---|---|
| 1/4 cup Crisco<br>1/4 cup flour<br>2 cups milk<br>1 teaspoon salt | Melt Crisco in saucepan; stir in flour. Add milk and salt all at once; cook and stir over low heat until thickened. Makes 2 cups medium sauce.<br>**Thin White Sauce:** decrease Crisco and flour to 2 tablespoons each; proceed as above. | **WHITE SAUCE** |
| | Add 1 cup shredded cheese to prepared sauce and stir until melted. | **CHEESE SAUCE** |
| | Brown 1/4 cup chopped onion in Crisco before adding the flour; proceed as above. | **ONION SAUCE** |
| | Add 1 tablespoon prepared mustard to sauce. | **MUSTARD SAUCE** |
| | Brown 1 cup sliced mushrooms in Crisco before adding the flour. Proceed as above. | **MUSHROOM SAUCE** |
| | Stir 1 cup cooked shrimp into prepared sauce. | **SHRIMP SAUCE** |
| 1/3 cup diced onion<br>1 slice bacon, diced<br>1 tablespoon Crisco<br>1 can (10 1/2 ounces) condensed beef broth<br>1/2 cup tomato puree<br>1/4 cup catsup<br>2 tablespoons diced carrot<br>1 1/2 slices white bread | In saucepan, cook onion and bacon in Crisco until tender. Stir in remaining ingredients. Cover; cook over low heat for 30 minutes. Press tomato mixture through a sieve; serve immediately or reheat to serve. Makes 1 1/4 cups. | **TOMATO SAUCE** |
| 1/2 cup chopped onion<br>1/4 cup Crisco<br>1 cup meat stock or 1 bouillion cube dissolved in 1 cup boiling water<br>1 cup catsup<br>2 tablespoons vinegar<br>1 tablespoon lemon juice<br>1 tablespoon worcestershire sauce<br>1 teaspoon salt<br>1/4 teaspoon dried oregano<br>1/8 teaspoon each sage, dried thyme, and tarragon | In saucepan, cook onion in Crisco until tender. Add remaining ingredients and simmer 15 to 20 minutes. Serve with chicken or spareribs. Makes 2 1/2 cups. | **HERB BARBECUE SAUCE** |
| 1 cup chopped onion<br>1/4 cup Crisco<br>1 cup meat stock or 1 bouillion cube dissolved in 1 cup boiling water<br>1/2 cup catsup<br>2 tablespoons worcestershire sauce<br>2 tablespoons vinegar<br>1 tablespoon sugar<br>1 clove garlic, minced | In saucepan, cook onion in Crisco until tender. Add remaining ingredients and simmer 30 minutes. Serve on grilled steaks, chops, burgers, or frankfurters. Makes 2 cups. | **ONION BARBECUE SAUCE** |

Cheese-sauced Zucchini Fritters could be an elegant luncheon main dish or an accompaniment to a roast beef dinner; use two cheeses to make the sauce doubly delectable.

When deep frying, heat shortening to 375° before adding the food. Then cook a few fritters at a time until golden brown. Use a slotted spoon to remove when done.

## ZUCCHINI FRITTERS

1 1/2 cups sifted flour
2 teaspoons baking powder
3/4 teaspoon salt
1 cup milk
1 egg, beaten
1 cup finely chopped zucchini
Crisco for deep frying

In medium bowl, stir together flour, baking powder, and salt. Combine milk, egg, and zucchini; add to dry ingredients and mix just until moistened. Drop from tablespoon into deep Crisco heated to 375°. Fry, a few at a time, until golden, 3 to 4 minutes. Drain on paper toweling. Makes 24 fritters. Serve with Cheese Sauce, page 85.

## TUNA ROLL

2 tablespoons chopped onion
2 tablespoons Crisco
1 tablespoon flour
1/4 teaspoon salt
1/8 teaspoon dried marjoram
1/8 teaspoon dried thyme
Dash pepper
1/4 cup milk
1 can (12 1/2 ounces) tuna, drained
1 tablespoon chopped parsley
1 egg, slightly beaten
Cheese Biscuit Dough
1 can (10 1/2 ounces) condensed cheddar cheese soup
1/2 cup milk
1 package (10 ounces) frozen mixed vegetables, cooked and drained

In large saucepan, cook onion in Crisco until tender. Stir in flour and seasonings. Add the 1/4 cup milk and stir until sauce thickens and bubbles. Stir in tuna, parsley, and egg. Roll out Cheese Biscuit Dough on lightly floured surface to 12x7-inch rectangle. Spread tuna mixture evenly down center of dough lengthwise. Moisten edges; fold dough toward center over filling. Seal edges. Place, seam side down, on greased baking sheet. Bake at 400° for 25 to 30 minutes. In saucepan, combine soup, the remaining 1/2 cup milk, and the vegetables; heat. Slice tuna roll; top with sauce.

**Cheese Biscuit Dough:** In mixing bowl, combine 1 cup sifted flour, 1 1/2 teaspoons baking powder, and 1/2 teaspoon salt. Cut in 1/3 cup Crisco and 1/4 cup shredded cheddar cheese until mixture resembles coarse meal. Add 1/3 cup milk; stir just until moistened and dough holds together. Place on lightly floured surface; knead about 8 times, until smooth.

## CHICKEN ORANGE AMANDINE

1/2 cup flour
1 teaspoon salt
1/4 teaspoon pepper
6 chicken breasts
1/2 cup Crisco
1 jar (12 ounces) orange marmalade
1/4 teaspoon ginger
1 tablespoon water
1/4 cup slivered almonds

Combine flour, salt, and pepper in plastic or paper bag. Add chicken pieces, a few at a time, and shake to coat. In large skillet, brown chicken on all sides in hot Crisco. Meanwhile, combine orange marmalade, ginger, and water. Place browned chicken in shallow baking dish and pour orange mixture over the top. Sprinkle with nuts. Bake at 350° for 1 hour or until chicken is tender; baste occasionally with sauce. Makes 6 servings.

## FRIED SCALLOPS

1 egg
1/3 cup milk
3 tablespoons Crisco, melted
1/2 cup flour
2 teaspoons sugar
1/4 teaspoon salt
2 pounds scallops
Crisco for deep frying

Combine egg, milk, and melted Crisco. Stir together dry ingredients; combine with egg mixture and beat until smooth. Dip scallops in batter and drain off excess. Fry, a few at a time, in deep Crisco heated to 375° until browned, 2 to 3 minutes. Drain on paper toweling. Makes 6 to 8 servings. Serve with tartar sauce.

## CORN STUFFED PORK CHOPS

8 pork chops, thin-cut
1 cup chopped celery
1/2 cup chopped onion
4 tablespoons Crisco
4 cups soft bread crumbs
1 can (8 3/4 ounces) whole kernel corn, drained
1/2 teaspoon sage
1/2 teaspoon salt
Dash pepper

Season chops with salt and pepper. In small saucepan, cook celery and onion in Crisco until tender; stir in bread crumbs, corn, sage, the 1/2 teaspoon salt and the dash pepper. Place half the pork chops on rack in shallow roasting pan. Spread evenly with stuffing; use about 2/3 cup for each. Top with remaining chops. Cover pan with foil; bake at 325° for 45 minutes. Remove foil and bake 30 minutes more or until meat is tender. Sprinkle with paprika. Makes 4 servings.

## VEAL SCALLOPINE

1 tablespoon flour
1/2 teaspoon salt
Dash pepper
4 veal cutlets (1 pound)
1/4 cup Crisco
1/2 onion, thinly sliced
1 can (16 ounces) tomatoes
1 can (3 ounces) sliced
   mushrooms
1 tablespoon chopped parsley
1 tablespoon capers, drained
1/4 teaspoon garlic salt
1/4 teaspoon dried oregano
Hot buttered noodles

Combine flour, salt, and pepper; coat veal lightly with mixture. In medium skillet, brown meat slowly in hot Crisco. Remove meat from skillet. Add onion; cook until tender but not brown. Add meat, tomatoes, undrained mushrooms, parsley, capers, garlic salt, and oregano. Cover and simmer until veal is tender, 20 to 30 minutes; stir occasionally. Arrange veal over noodles; top with sauce. Makes 4 servings.

## HUNGARIAN GOULASH

1/4 cup flour
1 tablespoon salt
1 1/2 pounds lean beef, cut
   in 1-inch cubes
3/4 cup chopped onion
1/4 cup chopped green pepper
1/4 cup Crisco
1 can (20 ounces) tomatoes
1 teaspoon paprika
1/4 teaspoon red pepper
1 cup carrot strips
1/2 cup chopped celery

Combine flour and salt; add beef cubes and toss lightly to coat. Add to large skillet with onion and green pepper; cook in hot Crisco until browned. Add tomatoes, paprika, and pepper. Cover and cook over low heat for 20 minutes or until meat is tender. Add vegetables and cook 20 minutes more. Drop Dumplings from tablespoon onto hot mixture; sprinkle with paprika. Cover; steam 15 minutes. Makes 6 servings.
**Dumplings:** Combine 1 cup sifted flour, 1 1/2 teaspoons baking powder, and 1/2 teaspoon salt. Stir in 2 tablespoons melted Crisco and 1/2 cup milk until blended.

## CHOP SUEY

1/4 cup flour
2 teaspoons salt
1/2 pound cubed veal
1/2 pound cubed pork
1/3 cup Crisco
1 cup chopped onion
1 cup celery, cut in 1-inch
   pieces
1 cup beef stock or boullion
1/2 cup soy sauce
2 tablespoons molasses
1 can (16 ounces) bean sprouts

Combine flour and salt; add meat cubes and toss lightly to coat. Brown in hot Crisco in Dutch oven; add onion and continue browning. Stir in celery, beef stock, soy, and molasses. Cover and cook over low heat for 25 minutes. Add bean sprouts; cook 15 minutes more. Thicken with additional flour, if necessary. Serve over hot cooked rice. Makes 4 to 6 servings.

## SUKIYAKI

1 pound beef round steak,
   thinly sliced across grain
1/4 cup Crisco
2 cups celery, cut in 1-inch
   pieces
2 cups fresh spinach, coarsely
   chopped
2 onions, thinly sliced
1 bunch green onions, chopped
8 ounces fresh mushrooms,
   sliced
2 cans (5 ounces each) bamboo
   shoots (optional)
1 beef boullion cube
1/2 cup hot water
1/3 cup soy sauce
2 tablespoons sugar

In large skillet or Dutch oven, cook beef in hot Crisco until tender but not browned. Add celery, spinach, onions, mushrooms, and bamboo shoots. Cover; cook 5 minutes; stir occasionally. Dissolve boullion cube in the hot water; combine with soy sauce and sugar, then add to meat mixture. Cook 15 minutes more. Serve with hot cooked rice. Makes 6 servings.

A crisp mixed green salad is ideal to serve with savory Veal Scallopine and noodles. Complete the Italian feast with frosty bowls of spumoni ice cream.

## APPLE BUTTER CAKE

1/2 cup Crisco
1 cup sugar
3 eggs
1 cup apple butter
2 1/2 cups sifted cake flour
3 teaspoons baking powder
1/2 teaspoon baking soda
1/2 teaspoon salt
1/2 teaspoon cinnamon
1/4 teaspoon nutmeg
1 cup sour milk
1/2 cup apple butter

Cream together Crisco and sugar. Beat in eggs, one at a time; beat until fluffy. Stir in the 1 cup apple butter. Sift together flour, baking powder, soda, salt, cinnamon, and nutmeg. Add dry ingredients to creamed mixture alternately with sour milk. Pour into 2 greased and lightly floured 9x1 1/2-inch round layer pans. Bake at 350° for 30 to 35 minutes. Cool. Spread bottom layer with 1/4 cup of the remaining apple butter. Top with 1 cup Fluffy Frosting, page 5; spread to cover apple butter. Cover with top cake layer. Frost sides and top of cake with remaining frosting. Swirl remaining 1/4 cup apple butter on frosted top to give a marbled effect. Garnish cake with apple slices, if desired.

## COCONUT LIME CAKE

2 1/4 cups sifted cake flour
1 1/2 cups sugar
1 teaspoon baking powder
1 teaspoon baking soda
1 teaspoon salt
4 tablespoons butter or margarine
1/4 cup Crisco
1 1/2 teaspoons vanilla
1 cup buttermilk
4 egg whites
1/2 cup flaked coconut

In large mixer bowl, sift together flour, sugar, baking powder, soda, and salt. Add butter, Crisco, vanilla, and 3/4 cup of the buttermilk; blend at low speed of electric mixer until moistened. Beat 2 minutes at medium speed. Add remaining buttermilk and egg whites. Beat 2 minutes more at medium speed. Pour into 2 greased and floured 9x1 1/2-inch round layer pans. Bake at 350° for 25 to 30 minutes. Cool. Spread Lime Filling between layers. Frost sides of top of cake with Fluffy Frosting, page 5. Garnish top with Toasted Coconut.

**Lime Filling:** In medium saucepan, blend 3/4 cup sugar and 2 tablespoons cornstarch. Gradually stir in 2/3 cup water. Add 2 slightly beaten egg yolks and 1/3 cup lime juice; blend. Cook and stir over medium heat until mixture thickens. Remove from heat; stir in 1 teaspoon grated lime peel, 2 tablespoons butter, and 1 drop green food coloring. Cool.

**Toasted Coconut:** Spread coconut in a shallow pan. Toast at 350° for 8 minutes or until coconut is browned; stir occasionally.

## BUTTER-SCOTCH PARTY CAKE

1 cup (6-ounce package) butterscotch chips
1/4 cup water
1/2 cup Crisco
1 cup sugar
3 eggs
2 1/4 cups sifted flour
1 teaspoon salt
1 teaspoon baking soda
1/2 teaspoon baking powder
1 cup buttermilk
1 cup whipping cream

In small saucepan, heat and stir butterscotch chips with the water until melted; cool. In large bowl, cream Crisco and sugar until fluffy. Add eggs one at a time; beat well after each addition. Stir in cooled butterscotch mixture. Sift together flour, salt, soda, and baking powder; add to creamed mixture alternately with buttermilk; beat with electric mixer on low speed after each addition. Pour into 2 greased and floured 9x1 1/2-inch round layer pans. Bake at 375° for 25 to 30 minutes. Cool. Spread Coconut Pecan Frosting, page 27, between the layers and on top of cake. Whip cream; frost sides of cake.

*Fluffy Frosting is swirled with apple butter to top this spicy Apple Butter Cake. It'll be as welcome after school as after a party meal.*

*A generous dollop of whipped cream cheese and warmed burgundy cherries make Cherry Devilicious Cake perfect for a card party snack.*

## CHERRY DEVILICIOUS CAKE

1/2 cup Crisco
1 cup sugar
3 egg yolks
1 teaspoon vanilla
2 1/2 cups sifted cake flour
1/2 cup cocoa powder
1 1/2 teaspoons baking soda
1 teaspoon salt
1 1/3 cups cold water
3 egg whites
3/4 cup sugar

Cream Crisco and the 1 cup sugar until fluffy. Add egg yolks, one at a time; beat well after each. Stir in vanilla. Sift together flour, cocoa, soda, and salt; add to creamed mixture alternately with cold water; beat well after each addition. Beat egg whites until soft peaks form; gradually add the 3/4 cup sugar; beat to stiff peaks. Fold into batter until blended. Bake in greased and floured 13x9x2-inch baking pan at 350° for 35 to 40 minutes. Cool. Cut into squares. Top each serving with a dollop of Cream Cheese Topper and warm Cherry Sauce.

**Cream Cheese Topper:** In small mixer bowl, beat together one 8-ounce package softened cream cheese, 1/4 cup sugar, and 2 tablespoons milk until fluffy.

**Cherry Sauce:** Drain 1 can (29 ounces) pitted dark sweet cherries; reserve syrup. In small saucepan, combine 1/4 cup sugar and 2 tablespoons cornstarch. Stir in reserved syrup. Cook and stir until thickened and bubbly. Remove from heat; stir in cherries and 1/4 cup burgundy (or 1/4 cup water and 1/2 teaspoon almond extract).

## DANISH PASTRY APPLE BARS

2 1/2 cups sifted flour
1 teaspoon salt
1 cup Crisco
1 egg yolk
Milk
1 cup cornflakes
8 to 10 tart apples, pared and
   sliced (8 cups)
3/4 to 1 cup sugar
1 teaspoon cinnamon
1 egg white

In medium bowl, combine flour and salt. Cut in Crisco. Beat egg yolk in measuring cup; add enough milk to make 2/3 cup liquid; mix well. Stir egg mixture into flour mixture. On floured surface, roll half the dough to 17x12 inch rectangle. Line a 15 1/2x10 1/2x1-inch baking pan with half the pastry. Sprinkle with cornflakes; top with apples. Combine sugar and cinnamon; sprinkle over apples. Roll remaining dough to make top crust; place over apples. Seal edges of dough; cut slits in top for escape of steam. Beat egg white until frothy; brush on crust. Bake at 375° for 50 minutes. While still warm, drizzle with Confectioners Sugar Glaze, page 27. Cut in bars. Makes 3 dozen.

## TWO LAYER BROWNIES

1/3 cup Crisco
1 cup sugar
2 eggs
1/2 cup sifted flour
1/2 teaspoon baking powder
1/2 teaspoon salt
1 cup chopped nuts
1 teaspoon vanilla
1 1/2 squares (1 1/2 ounces)
   chocolate, melted

In bowl, cream Crisco, sugar, and eggs. Sift together dry ingredients; stir into creamed mixture. Add nuts and vanilla. Divide batter in half. Add chocolate to one half and spread in greased 8x8x2-inch square baking pan. Spread the remaining light batter over dark. Bake at 375° for 20 minutes or until done. Cut in 16 squares.

## CARAMEL CUSTARD PIE

Crisco pastry for 1-crust pie
1 can (14 1/2 ounces)
   evaporated milk
2 eggs
1 cup brown sugar
3 tablespoons flour
2 tablespoons butter or
   margarine

Line 9-inch pie plate with pastry. Add enough water to evaporated milk to make 2 cups. In a small mixer bowl, combine milk and eggs; beat until well mixed. In a large mixer bowl, combine brown sugar and flour; cut in butter until mixture resembles coarse crumbs. Add milk mixture to brown sugar mixture; beat until well blended. Pour filling into pastry-lined pie plate. Bake at 400° for 30 minutes or until knife inserted just off center comes out clean. Cool.

*Raisin Cinnamon Rolls are as good a reason as any for gathering at coffee time; or serve for brunch with bacon omelet and a chilled fruit compote.*

## RAISIN CINNAMON ROLLS

3 1/2 cups sifted flour
1 package active dry yeast
1 1/4 cups milk
1/4 cup sugar
1/4 cup Crisco
1 teaspoon salt
1 egg
1/2 cup sugar
4 tablespoons butter or
   margarine, melted
2 teaspoons cinnamon
1/2 cup raisins

In mixer bowl, combine 2 cups of the flour and the yeast. In saucepan, heat together milk, the 1/4 cup sugar, the Crisco, and salt just until warm; stir to melt Crisco. Add to dry ingredients in mixer bowl; add egg. Beat at low speed of electric mixer for 1/2 minute; scrape sides of bowl constantly. Beat 3 minutes at high speed. By hand, stir in enough of the remaining flour to make a soft dough. Place in greased bowl; turn once to grease surface. Cover; let rise until double, 1 1/2 to 2 hours. Turn out on floured surface; divide dough in half. Roll each half to 16x8-inch rectangle. In small bowl, combine the 1/2 cup sugar, the butter, and cinnamon. Spread half the mixture over each rectangle. Top with raisins. Roll up, jelly roll fashion; start with long side. Seal long edge; cut in 1-inch slices. Place, cut side down, in 2 greased 9x9x2-inch baking pans. Cover; let rise until double, 30 to 40 minutes. Bake at 375° for 20 to 25 minutes. Drizzle with Confectioners Sugar Glaze, page 27, if desired, before serving.

## ORANGE BOWKNOTS

4 1/2 to 5 cups sifted flour
1 package active dry yeast
1 1/4 cups milk
1/2 cup Crisco
1/3 cup sugar
1 teaspoon salt
2 eggs
2 tablespoons grated orange
   peel
1/4 cup orange juice

In mixer bowl, combine 2 3/4 cups of the flour and the yeast. In saucepan, heat together milk, Crisco, sugar, and salt just until warm; stir to melt Crisco. Add to dry ingredients in mixer bowl; add eggs. Beat at low speed of electric mixer for 1/2 minute; scrape sides of bowl constantly. Beat 3 minutes at high speed. By hand, stir in orange peel and juice, and enough of the remaining flour to make a soft dough. Cover; let rest 10 minutes. Turn out on lightly floured surface. Knead until smooth, 8 to 10 minutes. Place dough in greased bowl; turn once to grease surface. Cover; let rise until double, 2 hours. Punch down; let rest 10 minutes. Roll dough on lightly floured surface to 18x10-inch rectangle. Cut in strips 10 inches long and 3/4 inch wide. Roll each into a rope; loosely tie in knot. Arrange on greased baking sheet. Cover; let rise until double, 45 minutes. Bake at 400° for 12 minutes. Makes 2 dozen. Frost with **Orange Icing:** Blend 1 teaspoon grated orange peel, 2 tablespoons orange juice, and 1 cup confectioners sugar.

## APRICOT ALMOND COFFEE CAKE

3/4 cup dried apricots,
   chopped
1/4 cup Crisco
3/4 cup granulated sugar
1 egg
1 1/2 cups sifted flour
2 teaspoons baking powder
3/4 teaspoon salt
1/2 teaspoon cinnamon
1/2 cup brown sugar
1/3 cup flour
4 tablespoons butter or
   margarine
1/3 cup chopped almonds

In saucepan, combine apricots and 1 cup water. Simmer, uncovered, 15 minutes; cool. Drain; reserve liquids; add enough water to make 1/2 cup liquid. In large mixer bowl, cream together Crisco and granulated sugar. Add egg and beat well. Sift together the 1 1/2 cups flour, baking powder, salt, and cinnamon. Add to creamed mixture alternately with the milk mixture; beat well. Stir in apricots. Pour into a greased 9x1 1/2-inch round layer pan or a 9x9x2-inch baking pan. In small bowl, combine brown sugar and the 1/3 cup flour; cut in butter until crumbly; add almonds. Sprinkle mixture over batter in pan. Bake at 350° for 40 to 45 minutes. Serve warm.

## STROGANOFF FOR A CROWD

8 pounds beef round steak
1/4 cup Crisco
1/4 teaspoon pepper
2 cups chopped onion
2 cloves garlic, minced
2 cans (6 ounces each) sliced
   mushrooms
4 cans (10 1/2 ounces each)
   condensed cream of
   mushroom soup
1 can (10 1/2 ounces)
   condensed beef broth
1 can (6 ounces) tomato paste
3 cups dairy sour cream
18 ounces noodles, cooked

Partially freeze meat for easier cutting. Cut meat into 2x1/2-inch strips. In large pan or Dutch oven, brown meat in hot Crisco, a pound at a time. Return all meat to pan; sprinkle with pepper. Add onion, garlic, and mushrooms. Combine soup, broth, and tomato paste; blend until smooth. Add to meat. Cover; simmer until meat is tender, about 1 1/4 hours; stir occasionally. Stir some of hot mixture into sour cream; return to hot mixture. Heat through, but don't boil. Serve meat mixture over hot noodles. Makes 24 servings.

## SPAGHETTI SAUCE

4 pounds ground beef
2 1/2 cups chopped onion
1 cup Crisco
4 cans (16 ounces each)
   tomatoes
4 cans (8 ounces each) tomato
   sauce
4 cans (6 ounces each) tomato
   paste
4 cans (4 ounces each) sliced
   mushrooms
2 tablespoons salt
2 teaspoons dried oregano
1 teaspoon pepper
1/2 teaspoon dried basil
1/2 teaspoon dried thyme
4 cloves garlic, minced
4 cups (16 ounces) shredded
   cheddar cheese
4 pounds spaghetti, cooked

In large saucepan, cook beef and onion in hot Crisco until browned. Add remaining ingredients except cheese and spaghetti. Cover and cook over moderately low heat for about 1 hour. Stir in cheese and heat until melted. Serve meat sauce over hot cooked spaghetti. Makes 24 servings.

## TUNA NOODLE CASSEROLE

16 ounces noodles
6 tablespoons Crisco
6 tablespoons flour
6 cups milk
6 cups tuna, flaked
6 cups peas, cooked
2/3 cup pimiento, chopped
2/3 cup olives, sliced
2 teaspoons salt
1 teaspoon pepper
2 cups cornflakes

Cook noodles in boiling salted water according to package directions; drain. In saucepan, melt Crisco. Stir in flour; add milk all at once. Cook and stir until thickened and bubbly. Combine tuna, drained cooked peas, pimiento, olives, salt, and pepper. Arrange alternate layers of noodles and tuna mixture in two greased 13x9x2-inch baking pans. (Or, use four 9x9x2-inch square pans.) Sprinkle cornflakes over all. Bake at 350° for 1 hour. Makes 24 servings.

## APPLE CHEESE CRISP

16 to 20 medium apples
   (6 pounds)
2 teaspoons cinnamon
4 teaspoons lemon juice
3 cups sugar
2 cups sifted flour
1/2 teaspoon salt
1 cup Crisco
6 cups (24 ounces) shredded
   process American cheese

Pare, core, and slice apples into four greased 12x8x2-inch baking dishes. (Or, use four 2-quart casseroles.) Sprinkle with cinnamon. Combine 3/4 cup water and the lemon juice; pour over apples. Mix sugar, flour, and salt; cut in Crisco until crumbly. Lightly stir in cheese. Sprinkle mixture over apples in baking dishes. Bake at 350° for 30 minutes or until topping is browned and apples are tender. Makes 24 servings.

## COOKING FOR A CROWD

Entertaining a large group can be easy and fun if you plan ahead carefully. Always consider your budget, the menu, your kitchen space and facilities, and how the meal is to be served.

**MENU.** Stick to recipes you're familiar with or those designed for large numbers; this isn't the time to serve anything delicate or complex. Always choose items that can be made or assembled in advance.

Don't plan to include knife-and-fork food unless you can provide table space for every guest. Instead, select meatballs, casseroles, or fork-tender foods that are easier to handle. Avoid salads that melt, especially if they must share the plate with a hot entree. Marinated vegetables, tossed greens, or relishes are better than gelatin salads. Choose rolls that you can pre-butter and desserts that cut and serve easily.

**BUDGET.** Give plenty of thought to the cost of the items you've selected. Perhaps you could stretch your meat dollars more with a different casserole, or a more thrifty dessert choice. Remember, too, that overbuying and waste when cooking and serving are costly mistakes when every penny counts.

**PREPARATION.** Check in advance to see what cooking equipment is available, especially if you aren't entertaining in your own home. If you haven't enough large pans or serving equipment, arrange to borrow or rent them.

Measure the refrigerator and the oven to be sure both can accommodate the large pans. Allow about two inches space around pans in the oven for even heat distribution. If you are using an industrial oven, allow additional cooking time for the large casserole dishes and the baked goods.

**SERVING.** For a crowd of about two dozen, buffet service is best. If your group numbers closer to fifty, consider individual plate service, where you can control serving portions closely.

Make a sketch of the buffet or serving area to be sure traffic will move smoothly and that adequate space is provided between dishes.

Seating all the guests around a table is ideal, but if table space is a problem, use large trays for lap-style dining. Avoid making plate-balancing or stand-up eating necessary. Serve dessert and beverage separately or have them at table places in advance.

# BRIDE'S CAKE

2 recipes Silver Cake, page 25
5 cups sifted confectioners sugar
1 teaspoon salt
3/4 cup Crisco
1/2 cup milk
2 teaspoons vanilla

*For Three-Tier Cake:* Prepare 2 separate recipes of Silver Cake batter. Place one recipe in a greased and floured 11-inch round layer pan. Divide the remaining batter between a greased and floured 9-inch round layer pan and a 7-inch round layer pan. Bake at 350° for 30 to 35 minutes. Cool.

*For Four-Tier Cake:* Prepare 2 separate recipes of Silver Cake batter. Bake each in a greased and floured 13x9x2-inch baking pan at 350° for 40 to 45 minutes. Cool. Use one cake for bottom layer. Cut second cake into 2 pieces, 9x7 inches and 9x6 inches. Place the 9x7-inch piece on the bottom layer. Cut remaining piece in two equal pieces, each 6x4 1/2 inches. Place one on second layer. Cut remaining piece in 2 equal pieces, each 4 1/2x3 inches. Place one on third layer. (Save last piece for bride and groom.)

Prepare **Ornamental Icing**: In large mixer bowl, combine confectioners sugar, salt, Crisco, milk, and vanilla. Beat at medium speed 3 minutes, then at high speed 5 minutes.

*To Decorate Cake:* Assemble layers. Use Ornamental Icing and a cake decorating tube to make flowers or fluted edges (directions usually come with the tube). Top cake with fresh flowers or a miniature bride and groom ornament, as desired.

# BETTER BAKING/PROPER FRYING

**You'll bake and fry like an expert with these handy tips
from Crisco's kitchen. We've also included up-to-date hints on
nutrition to keep your family fit, plus valuable
information on meal planning.**

Crisco is a premium quality vegetable shortening made from specially selected
oils. It is specially formulated to be suitable for a variety of uses, such as the
many recipes found in this book. Because Crisco maintains the highest quality
standards, you can rely on it to give consistent results in baking and frying.

Remember, Crisco can be reused up to 15 times for deep frying. Fry at 365° to
375°. Cool the used Crisco about 1/2 hour, then carefully transfer to another
container while straining through cheesecloth. Store in a cool place such as
the refrigerator. Reuse for frying only. Always add a little fresh Crisco next
time you fry to replace any used in previous frying.

Accurate measuring of all recipe ingredients is the first rule for cooking success.
Measuring utensils may be made of metal, glass, or plastic; choose the design
and material that best suits your needs. Liquid ingredients such as milk and
water should be measured in glass cups with pour spouts. Dry ingredients like
flour and sugar should be measured in individual cups. Use individual cups for
measuring Crisco, too. Scoop it from can to cup with scraper; press into cup
firmly, then level off with straight edge of scraper. Individual measuring spoons
are used for small amounts of both liquid and dry ingredients. Remember,
warped or dented measuring utensils result in inaccurate measurements.

Measure liquids in a glass measuring cup on flat surface. Bend down to read the mark at eye level. The cup has a spout for pouring and extra space above the highest measuring mark to prevent spilling.

Dry ingredients should be piled into measuring cup with spoon. Don't shake cup; level top with spatula's straight edge. Pack brown sugar firmly into the cup so that it will hold its shape when turned out.

To calculate volume of a utensil, fill measuring cup with water. Pour into pan and repeat until pan is full. Determine pan size by measuring between the inside edges of the utensil with a ruler.

*Mock Mince Pie should appeal to everyone;
spices, apples, raisins, and jellied
cranberry sauce replace the mincemeat.*
*Turn to page 78 for the recipe.*

# HOW TO CUT UP A CHICKEN

To begin with, one should buy and store chicken wisely. Choose 2- to 3-pound chickens for frying and larger birds for roasting. Wrap fresh chicken loosely in waxed paper or clear plastic wrap and store in the refrigerator. Wrap the giblets separately and refrigerate. Use whole chickens within 3 days; use cut up pieces within 2 days.

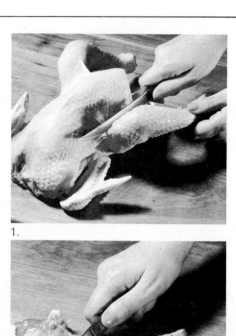

1.

2.

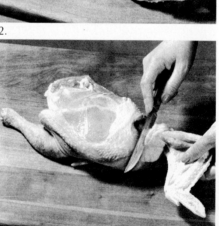

3.

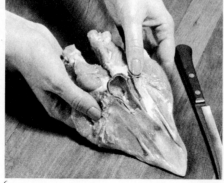

4.

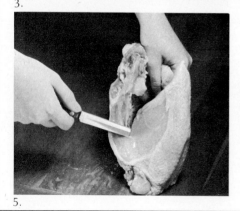

5.

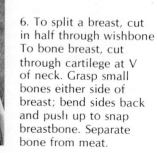

6.

1. Cut skin between thighs and body. Grasping one leg of chicken in each hand, lift until hips are free from body.

2. To remove the legs and thigh pieces, cut between hip joint and body close to bones in back of the chicken.

3. If desired, separate the thigh and leg. Locate knee joint by bending leg and thigh together; cut.

4. Pull wings away from body. Cut inside the wing just over joint; cut down through joint.

5. Divide body by placing bird on neck end and cutting along breast end of ribs to the neck. Separate breast and back section, cutting through the joints. Bend back in half to break at joint; cut.

6. To split a breast, cut in half through wishbone To bone breast, cut through cartilege at V of neck. Grasp small bones either side of breast; bend sides back and push up to snap breastbone. Separate bone from meat.

# FRYING TECHNIQUES

There are basically three ways of frying foods to crisp, tender doneness.

**Pan frying**—cooking in enough fat to cover the bottom of the pan and keep the food from sticking. Browning and sauteing are forms of pan frying.

**Shallow fat frying**—cooking in enough fat to partially cover the food but not suspend it or immerse it. As with pan frying, the food requires turning for complete cooking.

**Deep frying**—cooking in enough fat to submerge or suspend the food.

Always use the amounts of shortening recommended in the chart below. This insures foods with a tasty, crisp, brown crust and prevents moisture from escaping and food from sticking to the pan. If you're frying foods that are crumb-, flour-, or batter-coated, add at least 2 tablespoons extra Crisco for pan frying. A frying thermometer is important to help insure best results when deep frying. However, if you don't have one, a less accurate test for determining the temperature of deep fat is to drop a 1-inch square of bread into the hot Crisco. At 365° to 375° it should brown in about one minute. Fry frozen breaded foods like fish, onion rings, or shrimp, and frozen french fries without thawing.

Safety counts when you're frying. Watch the pan carefully when heating fat; bring to frying temperature slowly. If smoking occurs, reduce heat. Since overheated fat can catch fire, never leave the pan of fat on the range unless you can remain nearby. If you must leave the room for any reason, remove the pan from the heat. Remember to keep pan handles turned inward, rather than outward over the edge of the range. Wipe up any spills immediately. A tip to reduce spattering when frying frozen foods like french fries: shake or blot excess frost from the food before frying. Use a frying basket for deep frying.

|  | PAN FRYING | SHALLOW FRYING | DEEP FRYING |
|---|---|---|---|
| **SUITABLE FOODS** | Lean and tender meats like liver and veal; chicken; small fish and fish sticks; tender vegetables like potatoes and onions; dessert pancakes. | Small pieces of uncooked food like shrimp or breaded fish; large pieces of coated foods like chicken; potatoes, onion rings, cauliflower, eggplant. | Same meats and vegetables as for shallow frying; fritters and doughnuts. |
| **AMOUNT OF SHORTENING** | Use enough Crisco to cover bottom of pan and keep food from sticking; at least 1/3 cup in a 10-inch skillet for most foods. Some foods like chicken require about 2/3 cup for frying. | Use enough Crisco in skillet to partially submerge food, about 1/2 to 1 inch of fat, depending on the size of the food. One pound of Crisco makes 1 inch of fat in a 9-inch skillet. | Use saucepan 4 to 6 inches deep, 8 to 10 inches wide, or electric deep fryer. Fill no more than half full, about 3 pounds of Crisco. |
| **FRYING PROCEDURE** | Heat Crisco in pan on top of range or in electric skillet at medium heat. Add food and fry at recommended temperature. Turn and cook until done. Drain on paper toweling. | Heat Crisco in skillet to 365° to 375°. Add food and fry at correct temperature. Cook until done, turning food for complete cooking and browning. Drain on paper toweling. | Heat Crisco in pan to 365° to 375°. Add food a few pieces at a time, and fry at correct temperature. Cook until golden. Remove from fat with basket, tongs, or slotted spoon; drain on paper toweling. |

# PERFECT PASTRY EVERY TIME

Put a plus in your pastry next time. Add one of the
following to the flour of a single crust recipe:
1 to 3 teaspoons toasted sesame seed
1 to 3 teaspoons poppy or caraway seed
1 1/2 teaspoons curry powder
1/4 cup shredded cheddar cheese
1/4 cup finely chopped toasted nuts
1/2 teaspoon grated lemon peel
(and substitute 1 tablespoon lemon juice
for 1 tablespoon water, too).

## CRISCO PASTRY

**Single crust, eight or nine inch**
1 1/3 cups sifted flour
1/2 teaspoon salt
1/2 cup Crisco
3 tablespoons water

**Double crust, eight or nine inch**
2 cups sifted flour
1 teaspoon salt
3/4 cup Crisco
1/4 cup water

Sprinkle a few drops of water at a time over the flour mixture; toss with a fork. Then push moistened part aside and continue with remaining water and flour mixture.

For perfect pastry circles when rolled out, form the dough into a firm ball. With edge of hand, press dough three times across in both directions. Roll as directed.

Flute edge by pressing dough with forefinger against wedge made of finger and thumb of other hand. Cut slits in top crust. Lift the pastry by rolling it over the rolling pin; then unroll over the well-filled pie.

Combine flour and salt in mixing bowl. Cut in Crisco with pastry blender or two knives until mixture is uniform (mixture should be fairly coarse). Sprinkle with water, a tablespoon at a time; toss lightly with fork. When all water has been added, work dough into a firm ball.

**To make a single crust:**
Press dough into flat circle with smooth edges. On lightly floured board or pastry cloth, roll dough to a circle 1/8 inch thick and about 1 1/2 inches larger than inverted pie plate. Pick dough up and gently ease into pie plate, being careful not to stretch dough. Trim 1/2 inch beyond edge of pie plate; fold under to make double thickness around rim. Flute.
**To bake without filling,** preheat oven to 425°. Prick bottom and sides of crust with fork. Bake for 10 to 15 minutes.
**To bake with filling,** preheat oven to temperature stated in recipe. Do not prick dough. Bake according to recipe.

**To make a double crust:**
Divide dough into 2 parts and press into flat circles with smooth edges. On a lightly floured board or pastry cloth, roll bottom crust to a circle 1/8 inch thick and 1 1/2 inches larger than inverted pie plate. Gently ease dough into plate. Trim edge even with plate and add desired filling. Moisten rim of crust with water. Roll top crust the same way and lift onto filled pie. Trim 1/2 inch beyond edge of plate. Fold top edge under bottom crust and flute. Prick top crust.

**To make tart shells:**
Use empty 3-pound Crisco can as pattern for cutting pastry circles. Place pastry over individual pans, fitting closely. (Or fit over backs of muffin pans or inverted custard cups, pinching 4 or 5 pleats into the sides.) Turn edge under; flute. Prick with fork. Bake in 425° oven for 12 to 15 minutes.

# TOP CRUST VARIATIONS

A standard fluted edge is appropriate for any type of pie. To make one simply trim pastry 1/2 inch beyond rim of pie plate; fold under to make double edge. Then use thumb and index finger of one hand to make a wedge. Push dough into the wedge with index finger of your other hand. If you like, pinch curved edges into definite zigzags. For variety try one of the following suggestions:

**Zigzag edge:** Trim pastry 1/2 to 1 inch beyond edge of plate; fold under to make plump rim of pastry. Press dough forward diagonally with bent finger while pulling back with your thumb.

**Woven lattice top:** Place seven 1/2-inch wide pastry strips across filling. Weave first cross strip through center. Fold back alternate strips each time you add a cross strip.

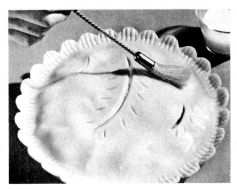

**Scalloped two-crust:** Trim crusts 1/2 inch beyond edge; pinch together. Cut scallops with tip of teaspoon, bowl side down. Mark each with tines of fork. Brush top with milk or cream.

**Shortcut edge:** Use pastry wheel to cut the zigzag edges of lattice strips. After sealing lower crust over lattice, press a double row of scallops with bowl of teaspoon.

**Can opener trim:** Make snowflake center with cookie cutter. For crust trim, press with beverage can opener, curved point side down. Sprinkle with sugar for sparkle when baked.

**Juicy pie edge:** Trim bottom crust 3/4 to 1 inch beyond edge of pie plate. Fold lower crust over latticed strips. Flute a high standard edge by pressing with fingers as shown here.

# YEAST AND QUICK BREAD TIPS

Home baked breads of all types are the pride of every cook and a favorite at any meal. Here are some tips for making picture perfect breads.

**Biscuits**—Cut the shortening into the flour, then lightly knead the dough to develop the flaky layers.

**Breads**—Knead dough lightly and allow enough time in a warm place for proper proofing (rising). To proof dough quickly, place the bowl of dough on a wire rack above a pan of hot water or else place the bowl in an unheated oven with a pan of hot water beneath it.

**Muffins and Nut Breads**—Avoid overbeating to assure tenderness and uniform shape.

## YEAST BREADS

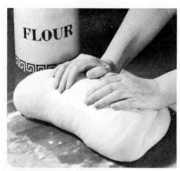

Knead dough on a lightly floured surface with lightly floured hands. Curve fingers over dough and push down with heels of palms. Give dough a quarter turn; fold over and push down again. Continue until dough is smooth, shiny, and elastic.

To shape the loaf of bread, flatten the risen dough with a rolling pin to a rectangle about 15x7 inches. Roll up towards you like a jelly roll, starting at the narrow side. Seal at each turn with fingertips or edge of hand.

Press down on ends of loaf with sides of hands to make two thin sealed strips. Fold the strips under the loaf, being careful not to tear the dough. Place it in loaf pan which has been greased. Your bread will have smooth crusts.

Test dough to see if it has risen enough to bake. Press it lightly with your finger, near the edge of the loaf. If the dent remains, dough is ready. Place in preheated oven. Be sure to leave room between pans for the heat to circulate.

## BISCUITS

Use a pastry blender or two knives to cut Crisco into dry ingredients for biscuits. Mixture should resemble coarse crumbs. Add milk all at once; stir quickly with a fork just until dough follows fork around bowl. Turn out and knead gently.

Roll or pat 1/2 inch thick. Dip cutter in flour; cut dough straight down. Place on baking sheet about 3/4 inch apart for crusty biscuits. For biscuits with soft sides, place them close together in a shallow baking pan.

# CAKE AND FROSTING CUES

Always use the pan called for in your recipe or check alternates below. If you don't know the pan size, measure pan across top inside the rim; mark the size on underside of pan permanently. Grease cake pans generously with Crisco before flouring lightly; fill pan half to two-thirds full with the prepared cake batter. Preheat oven 10 to 15 minutes before baking; keep pans at least 1 inch apart and 1 inch from oven walls. Baking powder may lose its leavening action with age. Test by adding a little to cold water; it should bubble actively.

Test a baked cake for doneness one of 3 ways. First, insert cake tester or wooden pick in center of cake; if tester comes out clean, cake is done. Second, look at cake's edges; if they are beginning to shrink away from the sides of the pan, cake is done. Third, touch center of cake lightly with your finger; if cake springs back, leaving no dent, cake is done. Cool cake layers in pans 15 to 20 minutes; cool loaf cake 20 minutes. Loosen edges. Place inverted rack on cake; turn over. Lift off pan and place a second rack on the cake. Turn again so cake is right side up.

To keep your serving plate clean while frosting the cake, place 3 or 4 strips waxed paper over the edges of the plate. Brush away any crumbs from cake. Put first layer on plate, upside down. Spread top with one-fourth of the frosting. Place second layer, right side up, on first layer. Holding spatula vertically, spread a thin layer of frosting around side of cake. Frost top of cake next, spreading to the edge. End by frosting sides with remaining frosting. Make peaks and swirls in cake top and sides as desired. Carefully pull waxed paper from under cake after entire cake is frosted.

Frost cupcakes the easy way. Simply dip the top of each cupcake into a fluffy type frosting (creamy frostings don't work well). Twirl the cupcake slightly and then quickly turn right side up. One recipe for a 9-inch layer cake also makes:
2 to 3 dozen cupcakes, or
one 9x5x3-inch loaf cake, or
one 13x9x2-inch oblong cake, or
two 9x9x2-inch square layers, or
one 10x4-inch tube cake, or
one 10x10x2-inch square cake.
Remember to adjust baking times.

For good nutritional balance select a variety of foods each day. As you plan meals, choose foods from the four food groups (meat, bread-cereal, milk, and vegetable-fruit), and include the recommended servings of each. You may then choose additional foods as needed to round out the meals.

### The meat group                                                    2 servings daily

These are the protein foods needed for growth and repair of body tissues. They also give us iron, thiamin, niacin, riboflavin, and other nutrients. You should have two servings a day from this group. One serving might be 3 ounces of lean cooked beef, veal, pork, lamb, poultry, or fish. Other foods that are high in protein and may be substituted for a meat serving are: 2 eggs; 1 cup cooked dried beans, dried peas, or lentils; or 4 tablespoons peanut butter.

### The bread-cereal group                                            4 servings daily

Whole grain, enriched, or restored breads and cereals are rich sources of thiamin, niacin, riboflavin, and other nutrients. Choose four or more servings from breads, cereals, cornmeal, crackers, grits, macaroni, spaghetti, noodles, rice, quick breads, and other baked products. You can count as one serving: 1 slice bread; 1 ounce of ready-to-eat cereal; 1/2 to 3/4 cup cooked cereal, rice, cornmeal, macaroni, grits, noodles, or spaghetti.

### The milk group                                                    2 to 4 servings daily

Milk is the primary source of calcium, needed for strong teeth and bones. It also is a good source of protein, riboflavin, phosphorous, and vitamins A and D. Adults should drink 2 cups of milk daily; children under nine, 2 to 3 cups; children over nine, 3 cups; teenagers, 4 cups. You can substitute: 1 ounce of cheddar cheese for 2/3 cup milk; 1/2 cup cottage cheese for 1/3 cup milk; 2 tablespoons cream cheese for 1 tablespoon milk; 1/2 cup ice cream for 1/4 cup.

### The vegetable-fruit group                                         4 servings daily

To provide vitamins C and A and certain other nutrients, four or more servings from this group should be included daily. Choose one rich source of vitamin C every day (oranges, grapefruit, cantaloupe, mango, broccoli, peppers, and fresh strawberries) or two fair sources (cabbage, potatoes, spinach, tangerines, or tomatoes). At least every other day serve a good source of vitamin A (apricots, broccoli, canteloupe, carrots, spinach, sweet potatoes, or winter squash). Remaining servings from this group may be any other fruits or vegetables you like.

Well-balanced meals don't just happen—they must be thought out in advance. Start with the main dish. Then choose breads, fruits, vegetables and other foods to complete the meal and to provide the nutrients your family needs for good health. Here are some tips to solve the meal planning puzzle:

• Choose foods with a variety of colors, shapes, and textures. You wouldn't want an all-orange meal any more than you'd want one that was all soft and mushy.

• Add a garnish that's an eye-catcher as well as a tasty addition to the daily fare.

• Accent bland foods with other foods that have a little zip or tang.

• Plan to have hot foods get to the table hot, cold foods cold; include some of each at every meal.

• Serve a light dessert with a hearty meal; save the rich desserts to complement the light entrees.

• Change your menu often, by trying new foods occasionally. A different seasoning or a new way to prepare an old favorite does a lot to make meals fun.

• Make the best of the time you have; foods you prepare ahead of time or cook together save time.

• Tailor meal costs to fit your budget by the types of foods you select.

## COOKING TERMS

**Bake:** to cook a meat or bread, etc. by dry heat in an oven.

**Beat:** to mix very well with a mixer, egg beater, or spoon till smooth. The motion lifts the mixture over and over, making it smooth and adding air to it.

**Blend:** to mix two or more ingredients thoroughly.

**Braise:** to cook slowly by moist heat in covered utensil in small amount of liquid or steam. Food can be browned in a small amount of Crisco before braising on top of range or in oven.

**Cream:** to beat Crisco and sugar together till fluffy and creamy.

**Cut in:** to distribute Crisco in dry ingredients by chopping with knives or pastry blender until finely divided.

**Dredge:** to sprinkle or coat with flour or other fine substances.

**Dry ingredients:** Ingredients in a recipe which are dry such as baking powder, soda, salt, flour.

**Fold:** to combine by using two motions, one which cuts vertically through the mixture, the other which turns over by sliding the implement across the bottom of the mixing bowl.

**Fry:** to cook in fat. Pan frying or sauteing is done in enough hot fat to cover bottom of skillet. Shallow frying is done in enough fat to partially cover food but not suspend or immerse it. Deep frying is done in enough fat to suspend or submerge the food.

**Mince:** to cut into very small pieces.

**Mix:** to combine ingredients till evenly distributed. Not as vigorous as beating.

**Pare:** to cut off the outside covering.

**Simmer:** to cook in liquid just below boiling point. Bubbles form slowly, not rapidly as in boiling.

**Stir:** to mix foods with a circular motion.

**Whip:** to beat rapidly to incorporate air and produce expansion. Generally applied to cream, eggs, and gelatin.